WILLIAMS-SONOMA

# NEW FLAVORS FOR
# soups

RECIPES
Adam Ried

PHOTOGRAPHS
Kate Sears

Oxmoor
House®

## spring

## summer

# fall

# winter

# introducing new flavors

It cannot be denied that the last two decades have been great for cooks and culinary enthusiasts. During this time, foods and flavors from all over the world have landed on our doorsteps. The tastes of Africa, South and Central America, Asia, and the Middle East have joined familiar French and Italian influences in our daily cooking repertory. Today, American pantries stock fragrant basmati rice in addition to the standard long-grain variety, pungent Asian fish sauce alongside yellow mustard, and spicy curry powder just behind the apple pie spice.

As if to keep international influences in check, a return to community has cropped up, along with our interest in cooking with seasonal and locally grown ingredients. The truth is, the passion and pride that go into carefully tended fruits, vegetables, dairy, and meats can be tasted, and this is one of the reasons why the movement toward buying local has taken such a strong hold. Not all of us have fruit orchards or dairy barns outside our doors, but, luckily, most of us have access to farm-fresh produce and dairy products at nearby farmers' markets, in good supermarkets, and sometimes through community-supported agriculture programs.

The forty-four soup and stew recipes in this book bring together both global and local forces right into your soup pot. Organized by season, the recipes in each of the four chapters focus on the very best produce of the moment—from the first tight-leaved artichokes of spring to the hardy leafy greens of winter—and turn them into dishes that satisfy our seasonal cravings. Balmy days call for chilled soups with bright flavors; the blustery cold demands slow, rich braises. In these pages, our beloved old standards take on international accents: In every spoonful are familiar flavors that comfort and exciting ones that taste deliciously new.

# freshness as an ingredient

If you are lucky enough to have a vegetable garden (or a kind neighbor who does), pluck a ripe, high summer, sun-warmed tomato from the vine. Wipe it off, take a bite, and try to compare that fruity, sweet-tart flavor to that of the hard, mealy orbs called tomatoes in the supermarket in January. There is simply no contest.

**local** The difference between produce grown in a neighboring county and the specimens that cross international borders to get to market is dramatic, to say the very least. Distance means time, and time is a foe to flavor. At the nearby farmers' market or roadside farmstand, the fruits and vegetables are likely grown within a few miles and were picked just hours earlier. Local farmers and producers invest their knowledge, expertise, and hearts into their goods. This attention has a flavor that can be tasted, one that gives a dish a running start to greatness.

**seasonal** Back to that January "tomato." Tomatoes are summer fruits, meant to reach peak sweetness and flavor after days in the hot sun. Summer, not winter, is the time to indulge. Each season has glorious ingredients for the soup pot—from grassy green garlic for a spring artichoke soup to post-frost kale for a winter soup with sweet potatoes and sausage. Cooking with peak produce gives your table a deliciously seasonal pace and gives diners an appreciation of time and place.

**organic** Pesticides and preservatives may promote long shelf life in fruit and vegetables, but they do no favors for our palate, our health, or the health of the soil that they're grown in. If you have the option, choose organic produce and meats free of such chemicals. By going organic, you are using minimally processed ingredients that taste the way that nature intended.

# being bold

By using the best-quality and fullest-flavored ingredients, each recipe in this book brings a bold statement to the table. Cooking techniques uncover or create flavor at every turn, while unexpected pairings of ingredients yield fresh new tastes.

**global ingredients** Today, star anise and Spanish smoked paprika have their spots on the spice rack beside such standards as cinnamon and nutmeg. What delicious fortune: We have a whole world of ingredients to explore, from Japanese miso to Mexican chiles to English Cheddar cheese. With these flavorings at our fingertips, old favorites find new identities—homey turkey soup gets flavor from aromatic jasmine rice; carrot soup is enriched with silky coconut milk; and lentil soup takes on meatiness from the addition of Serrano ham.

**flavorful cooking methods** The recipes tease every ounce of flavor from each ingredient, for example, from the shells left after peeling shrimp for gumbo and from the corn cobs that remain after cutting off the kernels for chowder. The deep browning of onions, the charring of vegetables on a grill, and the frying of tomatillo purée—these are all cooking techniques that create flavorful foundations on which to build soups with deep, resonating tastes.

**unexpected pairings** Even with a pantryful of new flavors, don't discount the potential of everyday elements to surprise when combined in clever, unexpected ways. Fresh ginger and cinnamon accent the richness of beef in a beef noodle soup with baby bok choy. Pesto is a go-to summer sauce for pasta lovers, but replacing tried-and-true basil with peppery arugula, and using the sauce to garnish a vegetable minestra with orzo helps us see the soup—and the pesto—in a new light.

# flavors in layers

A single flavor may taste good on its own, but try combining it with contrasting or complemetary ones—you'll be building complexity within the dish that engages diners' palates with every spoonful. For even more interest, think about bringing together different textures to add wonderful dimension to any soup.

**building complexity** The soup recipes here build intriguing layers of taste by finely balancing savory, sweet, salty, sour, hot, and sometimes even bitter, flavors. Caramelized onion soup, for instance, is sweet from the onions' natural sugars, but this sweetness is grounded by the savoriness of the beef and chicken stocks and the pungency of blue cheese croutons. Dry vermouth and fresh herbs tie together the flavors and smooth over any rough edges.

**the importance of texture** A soup would be inordinately dull if it was uniformly smooth or had chunks of only one chewiness. Texture is an important element, one that is often overlooked. Whether the textures complement one another, like buttery potatoes and tender leeks in rustic potato-leek soup, or contrast, like crisp cheese wafers with a silken tomato bisque, an appealing mix effectively stimulates the palate to make for a much more interesting bowl of soup.

We're in luck. The array of global ingredients that have become readily available to us are just what we need to revitalize old soup stand-bys. The recipes in this book use all the tools we have at our disposal to give every pot of soup a surge of flavor and texture. Keep these recipes in mind the next time you visit a farmers' market or walk down the international aisle of the grocery store: You will be at the threshold of great new flavors for all of your favorite soups.

spring

# leek and asparagus vichyssoise

**leeks,** 5 (about 2½ pounds total weight)

**unsalted butter,** 2 tablespoons

**canola oil,** 2 tablespoons

**fresh thyme,** 1 teaspoon minced

**chicken stock (page 142) or low-sodium chicken broth,** 5 cups

**russet potato,** 1 small, peeled and coarsely chopped

**asparagus,** 2 pounds

**baby spinach leaves,** 1 cup packed

**half-and-half,** 1 cup, plus 3 tablespoons for garnish

**kosher salt and freshly ground pepper**

MAKES 6–8 SERVINGS

Using a chef's knife, trim off and discard the dark green tops of the leeks. Cut the leeks in half lengthwise and then cut each half crosswise into pieces ¼ inch thick. Rinse well and drain.

In a large Dutch oven or other heavy pot with a lid, melt 1 tablespoon of the butter with 1 tablespoon of the oil over medium-high heat. Set aside 1 cup of the leeks and add the rest to the pot along with the thyme. Reduce the heat to low, cover, and cook, stirring occasionally, until the leeks are softened, about 10 minutes. Add the stock and potato, raise the heat to medium-high, cover, and bring to a boil. Reduce the heat to medium-low and simmer until the potato is tender, about 10 minutes.

Meanwhile, snap off the tough ends of the asparagus spears and chop the spears coarsely. When the potato is tender, add the asparagus to the pot, cover, and cook until the asparagus is bright green and just tender, about 3 minutes. Stir in the spinach and cook just until it wilts, about 45 seconds.

Working in batches, transfer the mixture to a blender and process to a purée. Pour the purée into a bowl. Add the 1 cup half-and-half, 1 teaspoon salt, and pepper to taste and stir to blend. Let cool to room temperature. Cover and refrigerate until well chilled, at least 4 hours or up to 12 hours.

When ready to serve, in a frying pan, melt the remaining 1 tablespoon butter with the remaining 1 tablespoon oil over medium heat. Add the reserved 1 cup leeks and ¼ teaspoon salt and sauté until the leeks are crisp, about 8 minutes. Transfer to a paper towel–lined plate to drain.

Taste the soup and adjust the seasonings. Ladle it into chilled bowls, drizzle with the 3 tablespoons half-and-half, dividing it evenly, garnish with the fried leeks, and serve right away.

*Leeks have a flavor that is milder, earthier, and yet somehow more substantial than that of their onion kin. Here, leeks pair with the grassy taste of fresh asparagus and the faint mineral nuances of baby spinach to create a quintessential springtime soup. Vichyssoise is usually served chilled, but if you prefer it warm, that's fine, too.*

# fish, fennel, and saffron stew with lemon aioli

*Saffron threads infuse this interpretation of Provençal bouillabaisse with its distinctive, slightly floral taste as well as a golden hue. Pernod, an anise-flavored liqueur, underscores the sweetness and licorice-like character of the fresh fennel in the stew. Aioli-topped croutons are perfect for soaking up the aromatic broth.*

Preheat the oven to 425°F. Cut the baguette on the diagonal into 16 slices about 1 inch thick. Brush the tops of the baguette slices with ¼ cup of the olive oil. Arrange them, oiled side up, on a baking sheet and toast in the oven until browned, about 7 minutes. Lightly crush 1 of the garlic cloves, and then rub each crouton with the crushed clove. Set the croutons aside.

Finely grate 2 teaspoons zest from 1 of the oranges, and then squeeze ¾ cup juice from both oranges. Mince the remaining 6 garlic cloves. Cut the fish into 2-inch chunks and season lightly with salt and pepper.

In a large Dutch oven or other heavy pot with a lid, warm ¼ cup of the olive oil over medium heat. Add the onion and fennel, and sauté until the vegetables are slightly softened, about 4 minutes. Add half of the minced garlic, the thyme, saffron, and orange zest and cook, stirring often, until fragrant, about 1 minute. Raise the heat to high. Add the orange juice, vermouth, fish broth, and the tomatoes with their juices and bring to a boil. Boil, uncovered, to blend the flavors, about 3 minutes. Reduce the heat to medium and add the remaining 2 tablespoons olive oil, the remaining minced garlic, the Pernod, and 2 teaspoons salt and stir to blend.

Place the fish chunks in the pot and gently push down on them with a spoon to submerge them in the liquid. Cover and cook until the fish is opaque throughout, about 10 minutes.

Meanwhile, top each crouton with a scant tablespoon of lemon aioli. Taste the soup and adjust the seasonings. Add the fennel fronds and stir gently to mix. Ladle the soup into 8 warmed bowls, garnish each serving with 2 of the aioli-topped croutons, and serve right away.

**baguette**, 1

**olive oil**, ½ cup plus 2 tablespoons

**garlic**, 7 cloves

**oranges**, 2

**skinless monkfish or mahi mahi fillets**, 3 pounds

**kosher salt and freshly ground pepper**

**yellow onion**, 1, cut into ½-inch dice

**fennel bulbs**, 2, cored and cut into ½-inch dice, plus ⅓ cup chopped fronds

**fresh thyme**, 1½ teaspoons minced

**saffron threads**, ½ teaspoon, crushed

**dry vermouth**, ¾ cup

**fish broth (page 142)**, 5 cups

**diced tomatoes**, 1 can (14½ ounces)

**pernod**, ½ cup

**lemon aioli (page 144)**

MAKES 8 SERVINGS

Green garlic is a springtime treat, offering a full, round garlic flavor without the heat of mature garlic. Buttery steamed artichokes are the perfect backdrop for green garlic's mellow flavor in a soup that pays delicious tribute to the season.

# artichoke and quinoa soup with green garlic

**lemon,** ½

**globe artichokes,** 12

**unsalted butter,**
2 tablespoons

**yellow onion,** 1, finely
diced

**green garlic,** 4, white and
pale green bottoms finely
chopped, tender green tops
thinly sliced

**fresh thyme,** ½ teaspoon
minced

**chicken stock (page 142)
or low-sodium chicken
broth,** 6 cups

**quinoa,** ¾ cup, cooked
(page 145)

**kosher salt and freshly
ground pepper**

**extra-virgin olive oil for
serving**

MAKES 6–8 SERVINGS

Fill a very large bowl two-thirds full with water and squeeze the juice of the lemon half into the water. Working with 1 artichoke at a time and using a chef's knife, cut off the top 2–3 inches, then trim the stem. Break off and discard 2–3 rows of the outer leaves. Using kitchen scissors, snip off any remaining thorny leaf tips, then drop the artichoke into the lemon water.

In a very large pot fitted with a steamer basket, bring 2–3 inches of water to a boil over medium-high heat. Lift the artichokes from the lemon water and add them to the steamer, cover, and cook until the bottoms are tender when pierced with the tip of a paring knife, 35–40 minutes.

Using tongs, transfer the artichokes, upside down, to paper towels and let drain. When cool enough to handle, pull off the leaves from each artichoke (reserve them for another use) and use a spoon to remove the fuzzy chokes from the hearts. Finely chop 10 hearts and set aside. Thinly slice the remaining 2 hearts and set aside separately.

In a large saucepan, melt the butter over medium heat. Add the onion and and sauté until softened, about 5 minutes. Add the green garlic bottoms and cook until fragrant, 3–4 minutes. Add the thyme, stock, and the chopped artichoke hearts, raise the heat to high, and bring to a boil. Reduce the heat to low, cover, and simmer to blend the flavors, about 10 minutes.

Transfer half of the mixture to a blender and process to a smooth purée. Return the purée to the pot. Add the cooked quinoa, 1½ teaspoons salt, and pepper to taste and place over medium-low heat. Cook gently, stirring occasionally, until heated through, about 10 minutes.

Taste the soup and adjust the seasonings. Ladle it into warmed bowls and garnish with the artichoke heart slices. Drizzle each serving with olive oil, sprinkle with pepper and the green garlic tops, and serve right away.

*The flavor of green garlic is mellow like roasted garlic cloves, yet fresh and verdant, rather like green onions. It is a full-flavored springtime accent in this earthy soup that combines nutty, nutritious quinoa and sweet, mild-tasting fresh artichokes.*

# hot and sour soup with black pepper and star anise

*The "hot" in this soup comes not from chiles, but from a generous dose of freshly ground black peppercorns. In addition to heat, the pepper offers a wide array of flavor nuances, from smoke, to wood, and even fruit. Star anise, with its warm, spicy hints of licorice, fits right in. Slightly malty Chinese black vinegar adds the element of sour in this dish of contrasting tastes and textures.*

In a bowl, soak the mushrooms in 1 cup of hot water until softened, about 30 minutes. Lift out the mushrooms and cut off and discard the stems, then thinly slice the caps. Pour the soaking liquid through a fine-mesh sieve lined with damp cheesecloth. Set the mushrooms and their liquid aside.

Trim the pork chop and cut it into thin strips. In a small bowl, whisk together 1 tablespoon of the soy sauce, 1 teaspoon of the sesame oil, and 1½ teaspoons of the cornstarch. Add the pork and toss to coat. Let stand at room temperature for 30 minutes. In a small nonreactive bowl, whisk together the remaining 3 tablespoons soy sauce, the remaining 2 teaspoons sesame oil, 2½ tablespoons of the cornstarch, the vinegar, pepper, and ¼ cup water. In another small bowl, beat together the remaining ½ teaspoon cornstarch, 1 teaspoon water, and the eggs until blended; set aside.

In a large nonreactive saucepan, combine the stock, ginger, and star anise and bring to a boil over medium-high heat. Reduce the heat to low, cover partially, and simmer to blend the flavors, 15–20 minutes. Meanwhile, drain the bamboo shoots and cut them into thin strips. Pat the tofu dry with paper towels and cut into ½-inch cubes. Add the pork with its marinade to the pot and simmer until the pork is opaque, about 3 minutes. Add the mushrooms and their soaking liquid, the bamboo shoots, and the tofu and simmer until heated through, about 3 minutes.

Stir the vinegar mixture, stir it into the broth, and simmer until slightly thickened, about 2 minutes. Stir the egg mixture, then drizzle it into the broth in a circular motion. Stir gently so that the egg forms thin ribbons. Remove the pan from the heat and let stand until the eggs are cooked through, about 1½ minutes. Stir in the green onions; remove and discard the star anise. Ladle the soup into warmed bowls and serve right away.

**dried shiitake mushrooms,** 8

**boneless pork loin chop,** 1 (about ½ pound)

**soy sauce,** 4 tablespoons

**asian sesame oil,** 3 teaspoons

**cornstarch,** 3 tablespoons plus ½ teaspoon

**chinese black vinegar,** ½ cup

**freshly ground pepper,** 2 teaspoons

**large eggs,** 2

**chicken stock (page 142) or low-sodium chicken broth,** 7 cups

**fresh ginger,** 3-inch piece, peeled and minced

**whole star anise,** 4

**bamboo shoots,** 1 can (8 ounces)

**extra-firm tofu,** 7 ounces

**green onions,** 6, cut into 1-inch lengths

MAKES 6–8 SERVINGS

By concentrating their natural sugars, long, slow cooking transforms pungent onions into an extraordinary base for a robustly seasoned soup. A fresh herb bouquet counters the onions' sweetness with a savory flavor and fragrance.

# caramelized onion soup
## with blue cheese croutons

fresh flat-leaf parsley,
3 sprigs

fresh thyme, 2 sprigs

dried bay leaves, 2 small

unsalted butter,
7 tablespoons, at room
temperature

yellow onions, 2 pounds,
thinly sliced

sweet onions such as
vidalia, 2 pounds, thinly
sliced

kosher salt and freshly
ground pepper

dry vermouth, ¾ cup

chicken stock (page 142)
or low-sodium chicken
broth, 4 cups

rich beef stock (page 142)
or low-sodium beef broth,
2 cups

baguette, 1

blue cheese, preferably a
sharp, tangy variety such
as roquefort, 6 ounces

MAKES 6 SERVINGS

Tie together the parsley and thyme sprigs and the bay leaves with kitchen string and set aside. In a large Dutch oven or other heavy pot with a lid, melt 3 tablespoons of the butter over medium heat. Add all of the onions and 1 teaspoon salt. Cook, stirring often, until the onions release their moisture, the moisture evaporates, and browned bits form on the bottom of the pot, about 45 minutes. Fill a measuring cup with 1⅔ cups water. Raise the heat to medium-high, add ⅓ cup of the water, and, using a wooden spoon, scrape up the browned bits from the bottom of the pot. Cook until the water evaporates and browned bits form again, about 5 minutes. Repeat, adding the water ⅓ cup at a time, until the water is gone.

After the final addition of water, add the vermouth, stir to scrape up the browned bits, and cook until the liquid has almost evaporated, about 4 minutes. Add the chicken and beef stocks, the herb bundle, and 1½ teaspoons salt and bring to a boil over high heat. Reduce the heat to low, cover, and simmer to blend the flavors, about 30 minutes.

Meanwhile, preheat the oven to 425°F. Cut the baguette on the diagonal into 12 slices about 1 inch thick. Arrange the slices on a baking sheet and toast in the oven until lightly browned, about 5 minutes. Remove from the oven and preheat the broiler. Crumble the blue cheese into a bowl. Add 2 tablespoons of the butter and, using a fork, mash to form a fairly smooth paste. Spread each baguette slice with a scant 1 tablespoon of the blue cheese mixture and return to the baking sheet. Broil until the cheese is golden brown in spots, about 1½ minutes.

Add the remaining 2 tablespoons butter to the soup and stir vigorously to blend. Remove and discard the herb bundle, then taste the soup and adjust the seasonings. Ladle it into 6 warmed bowls, garnish each serving with 2 of the blue-cheese croutons, and serve right away.

*This soup, sweet with caramelized onions and savory with beef broth and blue cheese, gets a touch of acidity and brightness from the addition of dry vermouth. Vermouth's lightly floral and herbaceous hints round out the contrasting tastes, yielding a full range of flavors.*

# leek and yukon gold potato soup with fried prosciutto

*As a garnish for this soup, the fried prosciutto pieces may be small, but their presence is anything but. Meaty and superlatively savory, the richness of the famous ham punctuates the oniony flavor of the leeks and the butteriness of the Yukon gold potatoes, creating chewy-crisp pockets of saltiness.*

Using a chef's knife, trim off and discard the dark green tops of the leeks. Cut the leeks in half lengthwise and then cut each half crosswise into pieces ½ inch thick. Rinse well and drain.

In a large Dutch oven or other heavy pot with a lid, heat the olive oil over medium heat. Add the prosciutto and sauté until crisp, about 6 minutes. Using a slotted spoon, transfer the prosciutto to a paper towel–lined plate to drain. Add the leeks and ½ teaspoon salt to the pot and stir to coat. Reduce the heat to medium-low, cover, and cook, stirring occasionally, until the leeks begin to soften, about 10 minutes. Add the thyme and flour and cook, stirring constantly, until the flour is incorporated.

Raise the heat to medium-high and, stirring constantly, slowly add the stock. Add the potatoes, bay leaves, and pepper to taste, cover, and bring to a boil. Reduce the heat to medium-low and simmer until the potatoes just start to become tender, about 6 minutes. Remove from the heat and let stand, covered, until the potatoes are tender all the way through when pierced with the tip of a paring knife, about 15 minutes. Discard the bay leaves and return the soup to a simmer over medium-high heat. If desired, use the back of a large spoon to mash some of the potatoes against the side of the pot and stir them into the soup to thicken it.

Taste the soup and adjust the seasonings. Ladle it into warmed bowls, garnish with the fried prosciutto and chives, and serve right away.

**leeks,** 8 (about 4 pounds total weight)

**extra-virgin olive oil,** ¼ cup

**prosciutto,** 6 slices (about 3 ounces), cut into ribbons

**kosher salt and freshly ground pepper**

**fresh thyme,** 1½ teaspoons minced

**all-purpose flour,** 2 tablespoons

**chicken stock (page 142) or low-sodium chicken broth,** 8 cups

**yukon gold potatoes,** 5 (about 2½ pounds total weight), cut into 1-inch chunks

**dried bay leaves,** 2 small

**fresh chives,** ¼ cup snipped

MAKES 6–8 SERVINGS

# carrot and coconut soup with curried almonds

**sugar,** 1½ teaspoons

**kosher salt and freshly ground pepper**

**ground coriander,** 1 tablespoon, plus ¼ teaspoon

**curry powder,** ½ teaspoon

**unsalted butter,** 3 tablespoons, plus 1½ teaspoons

**sliced almonds,** ½ cup, toasted (page 145)

**yellow onion,** 1, chopped

**carrots,** 2 pounds, peeled and thinly sliced

**unsweetened shredded coconut,** ¼ cup, toasted (page 145)

**ground ginger,** ½ teaspoon

**chicken stock (page 142) or low-sodium chicken or vegetable broth,** 4 cups

**unsweetened coconut milk,** 2 cans (14 ounces each)

**rice vinegar,** 2 teaspoons

MAKES 6–8 SERVINGS

In a small bowl, stir together ½ teaspoon of the sugar, ¼ teaspoon salt, the ¼ teaspoon coriander, and the curry powder.

In a nonstick frying pan, melt the 1½ teaspoons butter with 1 tablespoon water and the remaining 1 teaspoon sugar over medium-high heat. Bring to a boil, swirling the pan to blend. Add the almonds, stir to coat, and cook until the liquid is almost evaporated, about 45 seconds. Transfer to the bowl with the spice mixture and toss to coat the almonds evenly. Pour onto a piece of parchment paper, spread in a single layer, and set aside to cool.

In a large saucepan, melt the 3 tablespoons butter over medium-high heat. Add the onion, carrots, coconut, ginger, and the 1 tablespoon coriander and stir to combine. Reduce the heat to low, cover, and cook until the vegetables give off some of their liquid, about 10 minutes. Add the stock, raise the heat to high, and bring to a boil. Reduce the heat to low, cover, and simmer until the carrots are completely tender, about 20 minutes.

Working in batches, transfer the mixture to a blender and process to a smooth purée. Pour the purée into a clean pot. Add the coconut milk, vinegar, 1 teaspoon salt, and pepper to taste and place over medium-low heat. Cook gently, stirring occasionally, until heated through, about 10 minutes.

Taste the soup and adjust the seasonings. Ladle it into warmed bowls, sprinkle with the spiced almonds, and serve right away.

*The bright, lemon-like nuances of coriander set off two kinds of sweetness in this soup—a familiar, earthy sweetness in the carrots and a more exotic, tropical sweetness in the coconut. Curried almonds provide hints of heat and fragrant spice, as well as a welcome crunch.*

Elegant Japanese soba noodles have a nutty taste from the buckwheat flour that is used to make them. In a minimalist Asian-inspired soup, the flavor of sweet sea scallops, smoky *dashi*, and spicy, grassy watercress bring out the soba's earthiness.

# dashi with scallops, watercress, and soba noodles

**large sea scallops,** 1 pound

***kombu,*** two 4-inch-square pieces

**bonito flakes,** 1½ cups lightly packed

**buckwheat soba noodles,** ½ pound

**soy sauce,** 5 tablespoons

**mirin,** 3 tablespoons

**kosher salt**

**watercress,** 1 bunch, tough stems removed

MAKES 6–8 SERVINGS

Remove and discard the small side muscles attached to the scallops. Cut each scallop crosswise into thirds. Cover and refrigerate until needed.

To make the *dashi,* in a saucepan, combine the *kombu* and 8 cups water and bring to a simmer over medium heat; do not let it boil. As soon as the liquid reaches a simmer, remove and discard the *kombu.* Add the bonito flakes and stir to distribute. Remove from the heat and let stand, covered, until the bonito flakes sink to the bottom of the pot and the broth is fragrant, about 5 minutes.

Meanwhile, in another large saucepan, bring 8 cups water to a boil over high heat. Add the noodles, reduce the heat to medium, and simmer until tender, about 3 minutes. Drain the noodles, rinse well with warm water, drain again, and divide among individual bowls.

Strain the *dashi* through a fine-mesh sieve into a large heatproof bowl and discard the bonito flakes. Return the *dashi* to the pan and place over medium heat. Add the soy sauce and mirin and bring to a simmer. Add the scallops, reduce the heat to low, and simmer gently until the scallops are opaque throughout, about 3 minutes.

Taste the *dashi* and adjust the seasoning. Add the watercress to the bowls on top of the noodles, dividing it evenly. Ladle the *dashi* into each bowl, distributing the scallops equally, and serve right away.

*Feathery bonito flakes, a staple in the Japanese pantry, infuse their savory, smoky flavor into a broth called* dashi. *At once delicate and deep, briny and fresh,* dashi *is the base for this simple soup made substantial by the addition of sea scallops, watercress, and soba noodles.*

# chicken broth with carrots and herbed matzoh balls

*Dill is a traditional flavoring for comforting chicken broth and matzoh ball soup, but here, the grassy flavor of parsley and the gentle bite of green onions add to dill's fresh herbal accent. Carrot coins add a subtle sweetness and welcome flashes of color, and homemade chicken stock yields a soup with a full taste and texture.*

In a bowl, combine the matzoh meal, 1 tablespoon salt, and ¾ teaspoon pepper and stir to mix well. In another bowl, lightly beat 3 of the eggs, then beat in the ⅔ cup stock, the oil, 2 tablespoons of the dill, the parsley, and green onions. Separate the remaining 3 eggs, placing the whites in a clean bowl and adding the yolks to the egg-herb mixture. Whisk the egg-herb mixture to combine, then add the matzoh mixture and stir to blend well.

Using an electric mixer on medium-high speed, beat the egg whites until stiff peaks form. Fold about one-quarter of the egg whites into the matzoh mixture to lighten it, then fold in the remaining whites until no trace of white remains. Cover and refrigerate for at least 2 hours or up to 8 hours.

Bring a large, wide pot of water to a boil over high heat and stir in 1 tablespoon salt. Wet your hands lightly and scoop up a scant 3 tablespoons of the matzoh dough. Roll the dough into a ball (it should be about 1½ inches in diameter) and set it on a large plate. Repeat to make a total of 24 matzoh balls.

Carefully drop the matzoh balls into the boiling water. Reduce the heat to medium-low, cover partially, and simmer until the matzoh balls float to the surface and are tender all the way through when pierced with the tip of a paring knife, about 1 hour and 15 minutes.

Towards the end of the matzoh-ball cooking time, in a large saucepan, bring the 10 cups stock to a boil over high heat. Add the carrots, reduce the heat to medium-low, and simmer until the carrots are tender, about 5 minutes. Add the remaining 2 tablespoons dill.

Taste the broth and adjust the seasonings. To serve, using a slotted spoon, transfer 3 matzoh balls to each of 8 warmed bowls. Ladle the hot broth over the matzoh balls, distributing the carrots equally, sprinkle with dill leaves, and serve right away.

**matzoh meal,** 1½ cups

**kosher salt and freshly ground pepper**

**large eggs,** 6

**chicken stock (page 142),** 10 cups, plus ⅔ cup

**canola oil,** 6 tablespoons

**fresh dill,** 4 tablespoons minced, plus leaves for garnish

**fresh flat-leaf parsley,** 2 tablespoons minced

**green onions,** 3, thinly sliced

**carrots,** 4, peeled and thinly sliced

MAKES 8 SERVINGS

# chilled sour cherry soup with tarragon

**fresh sour cherries,**
3 pounds, stemmed
and pitted

**unsalted butter,**
3 tablespoons

**shallots, 4,** minced

**lemon zest, 2 teaspoons**
finely grated

**fruity red wine, 2 cups**

**cornstarch,**
2 tablespoons

**sugar,** ²⁄₃ cup, plus sugar as
needed

**kosher salt**

**fresh sweet cherries,**
1 pound, stemmed, pitted,
and quartered

**heavy cream,** ¼ cup

**fresh tarragon,** ¼ cup
chopped

MAKES 6–8 SERVINGS

Add the sour cherries to a food processor and process to a smooth purée. Pour the purée through a fine-mesh sieve set over a bowl and, using a wooden spoon, press on the solids to extract as much liquid as possible. Discard the solids in the sieve.

In a large nonreactive saucepan, melt the butter over medium heat. Add the shallots and sauté until softened, about 3 minutes. Stir in the lemon zest and cook until fragrant, about 45 seconds. Add the sour-cherry purée, wine, and 1½ cups water and stir to blend. Raise the heat to medium-high and bring to a simmer.

In a small bowl, whisk together the cornstarch and ¼ cup water and stir it into the simmering cherry mixture along with the ²⁄₃ cup sugar and a pinch of salt. Reduce the heat to medium-low and simmer, stirring often, until thickened to the consistency of light cream, about 4 minutes. Remove from the heat and stir in the sweet cherries. Transfer the soup to a nonreactive bowl and let cool completely. Cover and refrigerate until well chilled, at least 4 hours or up to 12 hours.

When ready to serve, taste the soup and adjust the seasonings with salt and sugar. Ladle into chilled bowls and drizzle with the cream, dividing it evenly. Using a spoon, gently swirl the cream into the soup. Sprinkle with the tarragon and serve right away.

*The herbal, anise-like flavor of fresh tarragon has a savory yet sweet quality that plays off of the almond-like nuances of late spring's fresh sour cherries. This first-course soup of Hungarian origin features a bracing sweet-sour theme that's meant to whet the appetite for the dishes to come.*

Lemon's bright, lively flavor is found in the fruit's colorful zest, while its acidity is in its juice. Together lemon juice and zest provide citrusy highlights for a sprightly soup featuring a quintessential spring ingredient: fresh fava beans.

# egg-lemon soup with fava beans and fried garlic chips

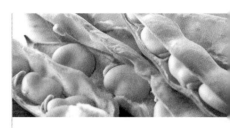

**kosher salt**

**fava beans in their pods,** 3 pounds, shelled

**lemon,** 1 large

**chicken stock (page 142) or low-sodium chicken broth,** 8 cups

**uncooked basmati rice,** 2/3 cup

**dried bay leaf,** 1

**olive oil,** 3 tablespoons

**garlic,** 6 large cloves, very thinly sliced

**large eggs,** 2, at room temperature

**large egg yolks,** 2, at room temperature

MAKES 6–8 SERVINGS

Bring a large saucepan of lightly salted water to a boil over high heat. Fill a bowl two-thirds full with ice water. Add the fava beans to the boiling water and cook just until the outer skins loosen, about 2 minutes. Drain the beans and immediately plunge them into the ice water. When the beans are cool, drain again and pinch each bean to remove its tough outer skin. Set aside.

Using a vegetable peeler, remove the zest from the lemon in wide strips. Squeeze 1/4 cup juice from the lemon and set the juice aside.

In the same large saucepan, bring the stock to a boil over high heat. Stir in the rice, lemon zest, bay leaf, and 1 1/2 teaspoons salt. Reduce the heat to medium, cover, and simmer until the rice is tender, 15–20 minutes.

Meanwhile, warm the olive oil in a small frying pan over medium heat. Add the garlic slices and cook, stirring often and watching closely so that they don't burn, until golden brown, about 3 minutes. Using a slotted spoon, transfer the garlic chips to a paper towel–lined plate to drain.

Using a slotted spoon, remove and discard the bay leaf and lemon zest from the broth mixture. In a nonreactive heatproof bowl, whisk together the eggs, egg yolks, and lemon juice. Whisking the egg mixture constantly, slowly ladle about 2 cups of the hot broth mixture into the egg mixture. Continue whisking until well blended, then stir this mixture back into the pot. Add the fava beans, reduce the heat to low, and cook, stirring constantly, until the soup thickens slightly and wisps of steam appear, about 5 minutes. Do not allow the soup to come to a simmer and remove it from the heat as soon as it has thickened.

Taste the soup and adjust the seasoning. Ladle it into warmed bowls, garnish with the garlic chips, dividing evenly, and serve right away.

*Delicate, buttery fava beans bring an air of spring to this spry soup inspired by the Greek dish called avgolemono. In it, the tartness of lemons balances the richness of eggs, while nutty basmati rice and toasty fried garlic add flavorful intrigue. If you have it, homemade chicken stock will give the soup a full, well-rounded taste.*

summer

# summer vegetable minestra with orzo and arugula pesto

**leeks,** 2 (about 1 pound total weight)

**extra-virgin olive oil,** 3 tablespoons

**carrots,** 3, peeled and finely diced

**celery stalk,** 1, finely diced

**garlic,** 2 cloves, minced

**fresh rosemary,** 1 teaspoon minced

**chicken stock (page 142) or low-sodium chicken or vegetable broth,** 4 cups

**ripe tomatoes,** 2 large, seeded and chopped

**parmigiano-reggiano rind,** 2-inch piece

**kosher salt and freshly ground pepper**

**orzo,** ½ cup

**green beans,** ½ pound, cut into 1½-inch lengths

**zucchini,** 1, cut into ¾-inch chunks

**arugula pesto (page 144)**

MAKES 6–8 SERVINGS

Using a chef's knife, trim off and discard the dark green tops of the leeks. Cut the white and pale green parts in half lengthwise and then cut each half crosswise into pieces ½ inch thick. Rinse well and drain.

In a large Dutch oven or other heavy pot with a lid, warm the olive oil over medium-high heat. Add the leeks, carrots, and celery and sauté until the vegetables are softened, about 7 minutes. Add the garlic and rosemary and cook until fragrant, about 45 seconds. Add the stock, 2 cups water, the tomatoes, and the Parmigiano-Reggiano rind. Raise the heat to high and bring to a boil. Reduce the heat to low, cover partially, and simmer to blend the flavors, about 20 minutes.

Stir 2 teaspoons salt and the orzo into the broth and simmer, stirring occasionally, until the orzo is still slightly firm, about 9 minutes. Add the green beans and cook until bright green and tender-crisp, about 4 minutes. Add the zucchini and cook until tender, about 3 minutes. Remove and discard the Parmigiano-Reggiano rind.

Taste the soup and adjust the seasonings. Ladle it into warmed bowls, garnish each serving with arugula pesto, and serve right away.

*A piece of Parmigiano-Reggiano rind simmered slowly in a broth releases the rich, savory character of the cheese itself into the liquid. The result is a deep, incredibly complex background against which summer vegetables and peppery arugula pesto really shine.*

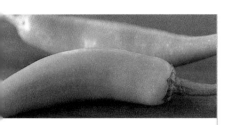

# chicken-coconut soup with summer squash and edamame

*The bright, sharp heat of fresh serrano chiles helps define the full range of tastes—sweet, salty, sour, and hot—in this Thai-inspired soup. The coconut milk–enriched broth is seasoned with spicy curry paste, pungent fish sauce, and herbal cilantro stems. Edamame retains its firm texture and sweet nuttiness with cooking, but slices of summer squash become tender as they soak up the flavor-intense liquid.*

Pull off and discard the dry outer layers of the lemongrass stalks. Using a chef's knife, cut off the tops of the stalks where they begin to toughen and discard them. Bruise the stalks with the flat side of the knife, and then thinly slice the stalks. Peel the ginger, cut it into 4 equal slices, and crush each piece with the flat side of the knife, and then crush the chiles in the same manner. Chop enough cilantro stems to equal about ¼ cup. Pluck ⅓ cup cilantro leaves and set aside.

In a large saucepan, combine the stock, 1 can of coconut milk, the lemongrass, ginger, chiles, cilantro stems, shallots, and 1 tablespoon of the fish sauce. Bring to a boil over high heat, then reduce the heat to low, cover, and simmer to blend the flavors, about 15 minutes.

Cut the squash crosswise into slices ¼ inch thick and set aside. Cut the chicken into thin slices and set aside separately. Strain the infused broth through a fine-mesh sieve. Wipe the pot clean and return the broth to the pot. Add the brown sugar and the remaining can of coconut milk and bring to a boil over medium-high heat. Stir in the chicken and edamame and return to a boil, then reduce the heat to medium and simmer until the chicken is almost opaque throughout, about 5 minutes. Add the squash and simmer until tender, about 2 minutes longer.

Meanwhile, cut 1 lime into 8 wedges. Squeeze 5 tablespoons juice from the remaining 2 limes. In a small, nonreactive bowl, whisk together the lime juice, the remaining 1½ tablespoons fish sauce, and the curry paste. Add this mixture and 2½ teaspoons salt to the pot and stir to blend well.

Taste the soup and adjust the seasoning. Ladle it into warmed bowls, garnish each serving with the reserved cilantro leaves, and serve right away with a lime wedge for squeezing.

**lemongrass,** 3 stalks

**fresh ginger,** 1½-inch piece

**serrano chiles,** 3

**fresh cilantro,** ½ bunch

**chicken stock (page 142) or low-sodium chicken broth,** 5 cups

**unsweetened coconut milk,** 2 cans (14 ounces each)

**shallots,** 5, chopped

**asian fish sauce,** 2½ tablespoons

**yellow summer squash,** 2 (about 6 ounces each)

**boneless, skinless chicken breast halves,** 1 pound

**light brown sugar,** 1½ tablespoons firmly packed

**frozen shelled edamame,** 1½ cups

**limes,** 3

**thai red curry paste,** 1½ tablespoons

**kosher salt**

MAKES 6–8 SERVINGS

Perfect summer peppers, fennel, and onions char and soften over the fire of a hot grill. The vegetables' smoky essence and natural sweetness highlights the gentle acidity of sun-ripened tomatoes in a spin on classic Spanish gazpacho.

# grilled vegetable gazpacho

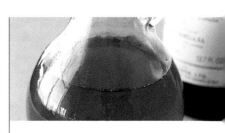

red bell peppers, 2

yellow onion, 1 extra large

fennel bulb, 1

extra-virgin olive oil for brushing and serving

english cucumber, 1

ripe tomatoes, 3 large

garlic, 2 cloves, minced

kosher salt

sherry vinegar, 7 tablespoons

good-quality tomato juice, 4 cups

ice cubes, 10

hot-pepper sauce, 1 or 2 dashes (optional)

fresh flat-leaf parsley, ¼ cup minced

fresh basil, 3 tablespoons minced

toasted garlic croutons (page 144)

MAKES 8–10 SERVINGS

Prepare a charcoal or gas grill for direct-heat cooking over medium-high heat (page 145). Replace the grill grate.

While the grill heats, cut each bell pepper lengthwise into 2-inch-wide pieces and remove and discard the stems and seeds. Cut the onion crosswise into slices ½ inch thick. Trim off and discard the top of the fennel and cut the bulb lengthwise into slices ½ inch thick. Brush the pepper, onion, and fennel with olive oil and arrange on the grill directly over the heat. Cook, turning occasionally, until the vegetables are softened and nicely grill-marked, about 10 minutes for the peppers and onions and about 15 minutes for the fennel. Transfer to a cutting board and let cool.

Trim away and discard the tough cores from the fennel slices. Cut the grilled vegetables into ¼-inch dice and place in a large nonreactive bowl. Seed and finely dice the cucumber, add it to the bowl, and toss gently to mix.

Core the tomatoes and cut them in half crosswise. Place a fine-mesh sieve over a bowl and gently squeeze the seeds from each tomato half into the sieve. Cut the tomato flesh into ¼-inch dice and add them to the bowl with the vegetable mixture. Stir in the garlic, 2 teaspoons salt, and the vinegar and let stand for about 10 minutes.

Meanwhile, using a wooden spoon, press on the tomato seeds in the sieve, extracting as much liquid as possible. Discard the seeds. Transfer the liquid to the bowl with vegetable mixture, then add the tomato juice, ice cubes, and pepper sauce, if using, and stir to blend. Cover and refrigerate until well chilled, at least 4 hours or up to 8 hours.

When ready to serve, stir the parsley and basil into the soup. Taste and adjust the seasonings. Ladle the soup into chilled bowls and garnish each serving with a drizzle of olive oil and a few croutons. Serve right away.

*A generous measure of sherry vinegar adds character to this spin on a classic——and incredibly refreshing——chilled soup. The vinegar's woodsy flavor highlights the smokiness of the charred vegetables while its fruitiness complements the sweetness of red, ripe tomatoes. Finished with fresh herbs, this simple no-simmer soup captures summer in a bowl.*

# egg and parmesan straciatella with baby spinach

*Farm-fresh eggs and nutty-tasting Parmigiano-Reggiano cheese conspire to give this simple soup a satisfying richness, while baby spinach gives it a vibrant color and verdant flavor. Just a few elements make up the soup, so use only the finest-quality ingredients you can find.*

In a large saucepan, bring the stock to a simmer over medium-high heat. Meanwhile, finely grate the Parmigiano-Reggiano cheese.

Divide the spinach among 6–8 soup bowls.

In a liquid measuring cup, mix together the cornstarch and 2 teaspoons water. Add the eggs and salt and pepper to taste and whisk lightly to blend.

Stir ⅔ cup of the cheese and the olive oil into the simmering stock. Stir the egg mixture and drizzle it into the stock in a circular motion. Stir gently so that egg forms thin ribbons, then remove the pot from the heat and let stand until the eggs are cooked through, about 1½ minutes.

Taste the soup and adjust the seasonings. Ladle it into the bowls over the spinach and serve right away. Pass the remaining cheese at the table.

**chicken stock (page 142) or low-sodium chicken broth,** 8 cups

**parmigiano-reggiano,** ¼-pound chunk

**baby spinach,** 4 cups lightly packed, roughly torn

**cornstarch,** 1 teaspoon

**large eggs,** 5

**kosher salt and freshly ground pepper**

**extra-virgin olive oil,** 2 tablespoons

MAKES 6–8 SERVINGS

Flavors from the sea and field make a delicious union when lobster meat joins summer's sweet corn. Not a drop of goodness is wasted here: Both the lobster shells and corn cobs are simmered into a broth that forms the chowder's base.

# lobster and sweet corn chowder

*Bacon enriches this luscious chowder with all of its smoky, salty goodness. Rendered bacon fat is used to sauté the onions, and then crisped bacon bits are added to the pot near the end of cooking. For briny-sweet lobster, tender summer corn, buttery potatoes, and silky heavy cream, there's no better match.*

Remove the meat from the lobsters, adding the shells to a large stockpot. Cut the meat into ½-inch dice, cover, and refrigerate until needed. Add 7 cups water to the pot with the shells and bring to a boil over high heat.

Slice 2 of the onions and add them to the stockpot; finely chop the remaining 2 onions and set aside. Remove the husks and silks from the corn and cut the kernels from the cobs (page 146). Reserve the kernels, then add the cobs to the stockpot along with the wine, tomatoes with their juices, parsley sprigs, 4 of the thyme sprigs, the bay leaves, and ½ teaspoon salt. Reduce the heat to medium and simmer for 1½ hours, skimming off any foam that rises to the surface. Strain the lobster stock through a fine-mesh sieve into a large heatproof bowl and set aside. Discard the solids.

Peel the potatoes and cut them into ¾-inch chunks. In a large saucepan, cook the bacon over medium heat until crisp, about 8 minutes. Transfer to a paper towel–lined plate to drain. Pour off all but 2 tablespoons fat from the pan and return to medium heat. Add the butter and the chopped onions and sauté until the onions are softened, about 5 minutes. Add the paprika and cook until fragrant, about 1 minute. Add the potatoes, the remaining 2 thyme sprigs, and 6 cups of the lobster stock (reserve any remaining stock for another use). Raise the heat to high and bring to a boil. Cover and cook until the potatoes just begin to soften, about 8 minutes. Using a wooden spoon, mash a few potato chunks against the side of the pan, stir them into the liquid, and cook until the potatoes are tender, about 5 minutes. Reduce the heat to low and add the lobster meat, corn kernels, bacon, 2 teaspoons salt, pepper to taste, and the cream and cook gently until the corn is tender and the lobster meat is warmed through, 6–8 minutes longer.

Taste the chowder and adjust the seasonings. Stir in the chopped parsley, top with croutons, if using, ladle into warmed bowls, and serve right away.

**maine lobsters,** 3, about 1½ pounds each, cooked (page 145)

**yellow onions,** 4

**fresh sweet corn,** 4 ears

**dry white wine,** 1 cup

**diced tomatoes,** 1 can (14½ ounces)

**fresh flat-leaf parsley,** 4 sprigs, plus 4 tablespoons chopped

**fresh thyme,** 6 sprigs

**dried bay leaves,** 2

**kosher salt and freshly ground pepper**

**yukon gold potatoes,** 5 (2½ pounds total weight)

**bacon,** 6 slices, cut crosswise into thin strips

**unsalted butter,** 2 tablespoons

**sweet paprika,** 1 teaspoon

**heavy cream,** 1½ cups

**toasted garlic croutons** (page 144; optional)

MAKES 6–8 SERVINGS

# tomato-bread soup
# with toasted garlic oil

**good-quality italian bread,**
1 pound, preferably
day-old

**extra-virgin olive oil,**
½ cup

**garlic,** 8 cloves, minced

**kosher salt and freshly
ground pepper**

**ripe tomatoes,** 6 large
(about 3 pounds total
weight)

**red onion,** 1 large, finely
diced

**carrot,** 1, peeled and finely
diced

**celery stalk,** 1, finely diced

**fresh flat-leaf parsley,**
4 tablespoons chopped

**chicken stock (page 142)
or low-sodium chicken
broth,** 4 cups

**parmigiano-reggiano rind,**
2-inch piece

**fresh basil leaves,**
6 tablespoons roughly torn

MAKES 6–8 SERVINGS

Cut the bread into 1½-inch cubes and set aside.

In a small frying pan, warm ¼ cup of the olive oil over medium-low heat. Add half of the garlic and cook, stirring occasionally, until light golden brown, toasted, and very fragrant, 12–15 minutes. Remove from the heat, stir in a pinch of salt, and set aside.

Core the tomatoes and cut them in half crosswise. Place a fine-mesh sieve over a bowl and gently squeeze the seeds from each tomato half into the sieve. Coarsely chop the tomato flesh. Using a wooden spoon, press on the tomato seeds in the sieve, extracting as much juice as possible. Discard the seeds in the sieve.

In a large Dutch oven or other heavy pot with a lid, warm the remaining ¼ cup olive oil over medium heat. Add the onion, carrot, celery, and 2 tablespoons of the parsley and sauté until the vegetables are softened, about 7 minutes. Add the remaining garlic and cook until fragrant, about 45 seconds. Stir in the stock, 2 cups water, the tomatoes with their juices, and the Parmigiano-Reggiano rind. Raise the heat to medium-high to bring to a simmer, then reduce the heat to medium, cover partially, and simmer until the tomatoes break down, about 15 minutes. Add the bread cubes, press down on them with a spoon to submerge them, cover, and simmer until the bread breaks down partially, about 10 minutes. Remove from the heat and stir in the remaining 2 tablespoons parsley, 2 teaspoons salt, and pepper to taste. Let stand for 2 minutes. Remove and discard the Parmigiano-Reggiano rind.

Taste the soup and adjust the seasonings. Ladle it into warmed bowls and garnish each serving with basil and a small spoonful of the toasted garlic and its oil. Serve right away.

*Slowly toasting garlic in oil softens its pungency, rendering it sweet and nutty. In this hearty summer soup, a drizzle of fruity olive oil infused with toasted garlic accents the bright flavor of ripe tomatoes and the wheaty, chewy artisanal bread. A sprinkle of herbs adds freshness and bursts of green color.*

# roasted yellow tomato bisque with asiago wafers

*Piquant, slightly fruity Asiago cheese takes on a toasty, caramelized flavor when grated and fried in a skillet. It forms lacy, irresistibly crisp wafers, the perfect garnish for this velvety soup that features sweet and mellow yellow tomatoes accented by the anise-like herbal undertones of fresh basil.*

Preheat the oven to 450°F. Line a rimmed baking sheet with aluminum foil. Core the tomatoes and cut them in half crosswise. Place a fine-mesh sieve over a bowl and gently squeeze the seeds from each tomato half into the sieve. Cut each half in half again and place the tomato quarters on the foil-lined pan, cut side down. Roast until the skins are brown and blistered, about 50 minutes, rotating the pan after about 25 minutes. Meanwhile, using a wooden spoon, press on the tomato seeds in the sieve, extracting as much juice as possible. Discard the seeds. Let the roasted tomatoes cool on the baking sheet. Slip off the skins and discard them.

In a large Dutch oven or other heavy pot with a lid, melt the butter over medium heat. Add the shallots and sauté until softened, about 3 minutes. Add the garlic and sauté until fragrant, about 45 seconds. Stir in the tomato paste and cook until fragrant, about 45 seconds. Add the stock, rice, and the roasted yellow tomatoes and their juices to the pot. Raise the heat to medium-high, cover, and bring to a boil. Reduce the heat to medium-low and simmer, stirring occasionally, until the rice is completely tender, about 30 minutes. Stir in 1 tablespoon of the basil.

Working in batches, transfer the mixture to a blender and process to a smooth purée. Pour the purée into a clean pot. Add the sherry, cream, lemon juice, 2 teaspoons salt, and pepper to taste. Place over medium-low heat and cook gently, stirring occasionally, until heated through, about 10 minutes.

Taste the soup and adjust the seasonings, adding the remaining 2 tablespoons basil and the sugar, if needed, to temper the acidity. Ladle it into warmed bowls, garnish each serving with 1 or 2 Asiago wafers, and serve right away.

**yellow tomatoes,** 6 (about 3 pounds total weight)

**unsalted butter,** 3 tablespoons

**shallots,** 5, minced

**garlic,** 1 clove, minced

**tomato paste,** 1 tablespoon

**chicken stock (page 142) or low-sodium chicken or vegetable broth,** 6 cups

**white rice,** $\frac{1}{3}$ cup

**fresh basil,** 3 tablespoons chopped

**dry sherry,** 1 tablespoon

**heavy cream,** $\frac{1}{2}$ cup

**fresh lemon juice,** $\frac{1}{2}$ teaspoon

**kosher salt and freshly ground pepper**

**sugar,** pinch (optional)

**asiago wafers (page 144)**

MAKES 6–8 SERVINGS

With their supple, watery crunch and melon-like hints, cucumbers are edible refreshment. Tangy yogurt and lemon, cool mint, and rich olive oil are lush-tasting counterparts in a chilled summer cucumber soup that will invigorate the palate.

# chilled cucumber-yogurt soup with lemon and mint

**cucumbers,** 6 large (about 5 pounds total weight)

**fresh mint leaves,** ½ cup minced

**extra-virgin olive oil,** 4 tablespoons

**lemon,** 1 large

**chicken stock (page 142) or low-sodium chicken broth,** 4 cups

**whole-milk plain yogurt,** 4 cups

**garlic,** 2 small cloves, minced

**kosher salt and freshly ground pepper**

MAKES 8–10 SERVINGS

Peel and seed the cucumbers (page 146). Finely dice 1 cucumber and place half of the pieces between layers of paper towels, pressing to absorb excess moisture. Transfer the dried cucumber to a small bowl, add 2 tablespoons of the mint and 1 tablespoon of the olive oil, and toss to combine. Cover and refrigerate until needed. Set the remaining diced cucumber aside. Cut the remaining 5 cucumbers into large chunks.

Finely grate the zest from the lemon, and then squeeze 3 tablespoons lemon juice. In a food processor, combine half of the cucumber chunks, 3 tablespoons of the mint, half of the lemon zest, and 1 cup of the stock and process to a coarse purée. Transfer to a large nonreactive bowl. Repeat with the remaining cucumber chunks, the remaining 3 tablespoons mint, the remaining lemon zest, and 1 cup of the remaining stock and add to the bowl. Add the remaining 2 cups stock to the puréed mixture in the bowl along with the reserved diced cucumber, the remaining 3 tablespoons olive oil, the lemon juice, yogurt, garlic, 1½ teaspoons salt, and pepper to taste. Stir to blend well, cover, and refrigerate until well chilled, at least 4 hours or up to 12 hours.

When ready to serve, taste the cold soup and adjust the seasonings. Ladle it into chilled bowls, garnish each serving with a spoonful of the chilled minted cucumber, and serve right away.

*A refreshing coolness is the dominant trait of fresh mint, but taste it carefully and you will detect an underlying sweetness, too. These flavors echo the same qualities in the cucumbers. Tangy yogurt and lemon are perfect foils to the cucumbers' subtle nature.*

# black bean and sweet corn soup with poblano chiles

*Glossy and deep green in color, poblano chiles have an earthy, vegetal flavor and just a suggestion of spiciness. Charred under a hot broiler, the chiles gain a roasted, almost smoky, taste and form the perfect backdrop for sweet corn, black beans, and fragrant garlic and cumin in this Mexican-inspired soup.*

Position an oven or broiler rack about 6 inches from the heat source and preheat the broiler. Place the chiles on a rimmed baking sheet and broil, turning occasionally, until the skins are charred, 10–15 minutes. Transfer the chiles to a bowl and cover. Let cool for about 15 minutes; the steam will loosen the skins. Remove and discard the skins, seeds, and stems from the chiles. Cut 2 of the chiles into thin strips and set aside; coarsely chop the remaining 3 chiles and set aside separately.

Remove the husks and silks from the corn and cut the kernels from the cobs (page 146). Discard the cobs.

In a large Dutch oven or other heavy pot, warm the olive oil over medium heat. Add the onions and chopped chiles and sauté until the onions are softened, about 5 minutes. Stir in the garlic, cumin, and oregano and cook until fragrant, about 45 seconds. Add the stock, corn kernels, and beans and stir to combine. Raise the heat to high, bring to a boil, and then reduce the heat to low and simmer to blend the flavors, about 20 minutes.

Transfer about half of the mixture to a blender and process to a smooth purée. Return the purée to the pot with the unpuréed mixture. Add the 1 tablespoon lime juice, 2½ teaspoons salt, and pepper to taste, stir to mix well, and place over medium-low heat. Cook gently, stirring occasionally, until heated through, about 10 minutes.

Taste the soup and adjust the seasonings, adding more lime juice if desired, then top with the roasted chile strips and red onion slices. Ladle the soup into warmed bowls and serve right away.

**poblano chiles,** 5 (about 1¼ pounds total weight)

**fresh sweet corn,** 4 ears

**olive oil,** 2 tablespoons

**yellow onions,** 2, finely chopped

**garlic,** 6 cloves, minced

**ground cumin,** 1 tablespoon

**dried oregano,** 2 teaspoons

**chicken stock (page 142) or low-sodium chicken broth,** 6 cups

**dried black beans,** ¾ pound, cooked and drained (page 145)

**fresh lime juice,** 1 tablespoon, plus lime juice as needed

**kosher salt and freshly ground pepper**

**red onion,** ½ small, thinly sliced

MAKES 6–8 SERVINGS

# charred eggplant soup with cumin and greek yogurt

**extra-virgin olive oil,**
1 tablespoon, plus oil for
grilling and brushing

**eggplants,** 2 large (about
2½ pounds total weight),
peeled and cut crosswise
into slices 1 inch thick

**ripe tomatoes,** 3 (about
1¼ pounds total weight),
cored, halved, and seeded

**carrots,** 3, peeled and
finely diced

**shallots,** 5, finely chopped

**garlic,** 3 cloves, minced

**fresh thyme,** ¾ teaspoon
minced

**ground cumin,** ¼ teaspoon

**fruity white wine,** 1 cup

**chicken stock (page 142)
or low-sodium chicken or
vegetable broth,** 5 cups

**kosher salt and freshly
ground pepper**

**greek-style plain yogurt,**
½ cup

MAKES 6–8 SERVINGS

Prepare a charcoal or gas grill for direct-heat cooking over medium-high heat (page 145). Replace the grill grate and brush it with olive oil. Brush the eggplant slices and tomato halves with olive oil and arrange on the grill directly over the heat. Cook, turning as needed, until softened and nicely grill-marked, about 8 minutes for the tomatoes and about 10 minutes for the eggplant. Transfer to a cutting board. When cool enough to handle, remove and discard the skins from the tomatoes. Coarsely chop all but 1 of the eggplant slices. Finely dice the last eggplant slice and set aside.

In a large Dutch oven or other heavy pot with a lid, warm the 1 tablespoon olive oil over medium-high heat. Add the carrots and sauté until just beginning to soften, about 4 minutes. Add the shallots, garlic, thyme, and cumin and cook, stirring occasionally, until fragrant, about 2 minutes. Add the tomatoes, coarsely chopped eggplant, wine, and stock and bring to a boil. Reduce the heat to low, cover partially, and simmer to blend the flavors, about 15 minutes.

Working in batches, transfer the mixture to a blender and process to a coarse purée. Pour the purée into a clean pot and add 1½ teaspoons salt and pepper to taste. Cook gently over medium-low heat, stirring occasionally, until heated through, about 10 minutes.

Taste the soup and adjust the seasonings. Ladle it into warmed bowls, garnish each serving with a dollop of yogurt and a few of the finely diced eggplant cubes, and serve right away.

*The supple texture of cooked eggplant is transformed into a soup that needs no cream to achieve its silken texture. Grilled eggplant slices assert their smokiness, shallots and garlic add pungent sweetness, white wine brings brightness, and a touch of musky cumin gives the soup an exotic flavor.*

Browning cooks off some of zucchini's moisture, bringing its delicate squash flavor into focus. Fragrant peak-season garlic mellows with sautéeing, but a measure of raw garlic in an herb garnish adds a kick to the summery soup.

# garlicky zucchini soup with basil gremolata

**leeks**, 3 (about 1½ pounds total weight)

**lemons**, 2

**olive oil**, 3 tablespoons

**zucchini**, 3 (about 1½ pounds total weight), cut into ½-inch dice

**garlic**, 3 tablespoons minced

**kosher salt and freshly ground pepper**

**celery stalk**, 1, finely chopped

**chicken stock (page 142) or low-sodium chicken broth**, 8 cups

**russet potato**, 1, peeled and finely diced

**fresh flat-leaf parsley**, 3 tablespoons minced

**fresh basil**, 3 tablespoons minced

MAKES 6–8 SERVINGS

Trim off and discard the dark green tops of the leeks. Cut the leeks lengthwise into quarters and then cut them crosswise into ¼-inch pieces. Rinse well and drain. Using a vegetable peeler, remove the zest in wide strips from 1 lemon.

In a large Dutch oven or other heavy pot with a lid, heat 1½ tablespoons of the olive oil over high heat. Add two-thirds of the diced zucchini and spread in a single layer. Cook, without stirring, until beginning to brown, about 1½ minutes. Stir to redistribute, then cook, stirring occasionally, until the zucchini is just tender, about 1 minute longer. Stir in 1 tablespoon of the minced garlic and ¼ teaspoon salt and cook until fragrant, about 30 seconds. Transfer to a large plate.

Add the remaining 1½ tablespoons olive oil to the pot and warm over medium-high heat. Add the leeks, celery, 1 tablespoon of the minced garlic, and ¼ teaspoon salt and stir to mix well. Reduce the heat to low, cover, and cook, stirring occasionally, until the leeks soften, about 10 minutes. Add the stock, potato, lemon zest strips, and remaining zucchini, raise the heat to high, and bring to a boil. Reduce the heat to low, cover partially, and simmer, stirring occasionally, until the potato is tender, about 15 minutes.

Meanwhile, to make the *gremolata*, finely grate the zest from the remaining lemon. In a small bowl, stir together the grated lemon zest, the remaining 1 tablespoon minced garlic, the parsley, and the basil. Set aside.

Using a slotted spoon, remove and discard the lemon zest strips from the pot. Use the spoon to mash the potato and zucchini against the sides of the pot and stir into the soup to thicken it slightly. Stir in the sautéed zucchini, 1 teaspoon salt, and pepper to taste.

Taste the soup and adjust the seasonings. Ladle it into warmed bowls, garnish with the *gremolata*, and serve right away.

Gremolata *is an Italian herb condiment with vibrant flavor and color. Here, basil takes the place of some of* gremolata's *usual parsley to add hints of licorice to parsley's grassy taste. Topped with this simple mixture, a garlic-infused zucchini soup gets a fresh, bold hit of summer.*

fall

# pumpkin soup with sweet and spicy pumpkin seeds

**sugar,** ½ teaspoon

**paprika,** ½ teaspoon

**cayenne pepper,**
¼ teaspoon, plus a pinch

**kosher salt and freshly ground pepper**

**unsalted butter,**
3½ tablespoons

**grade b pure maple syrup,**
7 tablespoons

**shelled pumpkin seeds,**
½ cup, toasted (page 145)

**yellow onion,** 1, finely chopped

**celery stalks,** 2, finely chopped

**garlic,** 2 cloves, minced

**dry white wine,** ½ cup

**chicken stock (page 142) or low-sodium chicken or vegetable broth,** 6 cups

**pumpkin purée,** 3 cans (15 ounces each)

**heavy cream,** ¾ cup

MAKES 6–8 SERVINGS

In a small bowl, stir together the sugar, paprika, ¼ teaspoon cayenne, and ¼ teaspoon salt. In a nonstick frying pan, melt ½ tablespoon of the butter with 1 tablespoon of the maple syrup and 1 teaspoon water over medium-high heat. Bring to a boil, swirling the pan to blend. Add the pumpkin seeds, stir to coat, and cook until the liquid is almost evaporated, 1–2 minutes. Transfer to the bowl with the spice mixture and toss to coat the pumpkin seeds evenly. Pour onto a piece of parchment paper, spread in a single layer, and set aside to cool.

In a large Dutch oven or other heavy pot with a lid, melt the remaining 3 tablespoons butter over medium heat. Add the onion and celery and sauté until softened and beginning to brown, about 7 minutes. Stir in the garlic and cook until fragrant, about 45 seconds. Add the wine, raise the heat to high, and bring to a boil. Cook until the wine is reduced to ¼ cup, about 2 minutes. Add the stock and pumpkin, stir to combine, and bring to a simmer. Reduce the heat to low, cover partially, and simmer gently to blend the flavors, about 10 minutes.

Add the remaining 6 tablespoons maple syrup, the pinch of cayenne, 2 teaspoons salt, and pepper to taste to the pot. Stir to mix, cover, and simmer to blend the flavors, about 10 minutes longer.

Meanwhile, add the cream to a bowl. Using a whisk or mixer on medium-high speed, beat the cream until it holds soft peaks.

Taste the soup and adjust the seasonings. Ladle it into warmed bowls, dollop each serving with a spoonful of cream, garnish with the spiced pumpkin seeds, and serve right away.

*Green-gray pumpkin seeds possess an intriguing squash-like flavor that sets them apart from other seeds and nuts. The seeds, like the meat of a pumpkin, take well to sweet partners, such as maple syrup, and to warm spices such as cayenne pepper that adds an undercurrent of heat to this autumnal recipe.*

# mussels in yellow curry broth with thai basil

*Mildly spicy Thai yellow curry paste (which has a reddish cast) gets its color and earthy taste from an abundance of turmeric, and delicious complexity from a panoply of other ingredients, including lemongrass, chiles, and shallots. In this recipe, yellow curry–spiced coconut milk combines with the briny juices released by the mussels as they cook, yielding a flavor-intense broth.*

Scrub the mussels and pull off any beards attached to the shells. Discard any mussels that do not close to the touch. Squeeze the juice from 2 of the limes. Cut the remaining lime into 6 wedges and set aside.

In a stockpot or other very large pot with a lid, warm the oil over medium-high heat. Add the shallots, garlic, ginger, and curry paste and stir to mix well and coat the shallots with the oil. Sauté until fragrant and the shallots are slightly softened, about 2 minutes. Add the lime juice, coconut milk, and fish sauce and bring to a boil. Add the tomatoes, half of the basil, and the mussels and stir to combine. Raise the heat to high, cover, and cook, stirring occasionally, until the mussels open, about 8 minutes; discard any mussels that fail to open after another minute or two.

Stir in the remaining basil. Spoon the mussels into warmed bowls, ladle some of the curry broth over the top, sprinkle with the cilantro, and serve right away with the lime wedges for squeezing.

**mussels,** 6 pounds

**limes,** 3

**canola oil,** 2 tablespoons

**shallots,** 8, thinly sliced

**garlic,** 6 cloves, minced

**fresh ginger,** 2-inch piece, peeled and minced

**thai yellow curry paste,** ¼ cup

**light unsweetened coconut milk,** 2 cans (14 ounces each)

**asian fish sauce,** 1 tablespoon

**ripe tomatoes,** 2 large (about 1 pound total weight), seeded and finely diced

**fresh thai basil leaves,** ½ cup torn

**fresh cilantro leaves,** ½ cup

MAKES 6 SERVINGS

A quick sauté of sliced cremini mushrooms helps to concentrate their meaty taste, the first step in building depth of flavor in a hearty fall soup. Porcini mushrooms extend the creminis' deep savoriness while farro adds earthy wholesomeness.

# beef and mushroom soup with farro

*Dried porcini mushrooms have a woodsy flavor and an intense earthy aroma that easily matches the richness of beef and even enhances its meatiness. Farro, with its nutty taste and chewy texture, adds yet another element of heartiness to this soup.*

Add the dried porcini mushroom to a heatproof bowl and cover with the boiling water. Let soak until softened, about 20 minutes. Lift out the porcini and slice thinly. Pour the soaking liquid through a fine-mesh sieve lined with damp cheesecloth. Set the mushrooms and their soaking liquid aside.

In a large Dutch oven or other heavy pot, warm 1 tablespoon of the olive oil over medium heat. Add the cremini mushrooms and sauté until the mushrooms give off their moisture and the moisture evaporates, about 7 minutes. Add the remaining ½ tablespoon oil, the onion, carrots, and thyme and sauté until the vegetables are softened and beginning to brown, about 7 minutes. Add the garlic and cook until fragrant, about 45 seconds. Add the reserved porcini mushrooms and their soaking liquid, the tomatoes, the farro, and the beef broth. Raise the heat to high and bring to a boil, then reduce the heat to low and simmer, stirring occasionally, until the farro is almost tender, about 20 minutes.

Add the shredded beef, 2 tablespoons of the parsley, 1½ teaspoons salt, and pepper to taste and stir to mix well. Simmer until the meat is heated through and the farro is completely tender, about 10 minutes longer.

Taste the soup and adjust the seasonings. Ladle it into warmed bowls, garnish with the remaining parsley, and serve right away.

**dried porcini mushrooms,** ¾ ounce (¾ cup lightly packed)

**boiling water,** 1 cup

**olive oil,** 1½ tablespoons

**cremini mushrooms,** ¾ pound, thinly sliced

**yellow onion,** 1, finely chopped

**carrots,** 3, peeled and sliced ¼ inch thick

**fresh thyme,** 1½ teaspoons minced

**garlic,** 3 cloves, minced

**canned diced tomatoes with juices,** ¾ cup

**farro,** 1½ cups, rinsed and drained

**rich beef stock (page 142),** 2 quarts, plus 2 cups shredded meat reserved from making the stock

**fresh flat-leaf parsley,** 4 tablespoons chopped

**kosher salt and freshly ground pepper**

MAKES 6–8 SERVINGS

# chicken-tomatillo soup with chipotle chiles

**corn tortillas,** 12

**canola oil,** 3 tablespoons

**kosher salt and freshly ground pepper**

**chicken stock (page 142) or low-sodium chicken broth,** 8 cups

**boneless, skinless chicken breasts,** 1½ pounds

**fresh oregano,** 1 sprig

**fresh cilantro,** 10 sprigs

**garlic,** 9 cloves, crushed

**tomatillos,** 1 pound, husked and chopped

**white onion,** 1, chopped

**chipotle chiles in adobo sauce,** 2 large, minced, plus 1 tablespoon adobo sauce

**fresh lime juice,** 4 teaspoons

**ripe hass avocado,** 1

**cherry or grape tomatoes,** 1½ cups, quartered

**cotija or feta cheese,** ½ pound, crumbled

MAKES 6–8 SERVINGS

Preheat the oven to 425°F. Cut the tortillas into ¼-inch strips and place in a bowl. Drizzle with 1½ tablespoons of the oil, sprinkle with ¼ teaspoon salt, and toss to coat. Spread the strips on a large rimmed baking sheet and bake until crisp and brown, about 15 minutes, shaking and rotating the pan about halfway through. Transfer to a paper towel–lined plate to drain.

In a large saucepan, combine the stock, chicken breasts, oregano and cilantro sprigs, and 3 of the crushed garlic cloves and bring to a boil over medium-high heat. Reduce the heat to low, cover, and simmer until the chicken is opaque throughout, 15–20 minutes. Transfer the chicken to a plate and let cool. Strain the broth through a fine-mesh sieve into a large heatproof bowl. Discard the solids in the sieve. Wipe out the pan and set aside. Shred the chicken into bite-sized pieces and set aside.

In a food processor, combine the tomatillos, onion, chipotle chiles and adobo sauce, and the remaining 6 garlic cloves and process to a smooth purée. In the clean saucepan, heat the remaining 1½ tablespoons oil over high heat. Add the tomatillo mixture and fry, stirring occasionally, until the liquid evaporates, the color darkens, and the mixture is fragrant, about 15 minutes. Add the broth and bring to a simmer. Cook, stirring occasionally, to blend the flavors, about 10 minutes. Add 1½ teaspoons salt, 3 teaspoons of the lime juice, the shredded chicken, and pepper to taste and simmer until the chicken is heated through, about 5 minutes.

Meanwhile, pit, peel, and dice the avocado, then place it in a small serving bowl and toss with the remaining 1 teaspoon lime juice. Place the tomatoes and cheese in separate small serving bowls.

Taste the soup and adjust the seasonings. Ladle it into warmed bowls, top with the tortilla strips, and serve right away. Pass the avocado, tomatoes, and cheese at the table.

*Chipotle chiles in adobo sauce add character at many levels here—the chiles themselves add smokiness and, of course, heat, while the adobo sauce lends a sweet-tartness and even more spiciness. Tangy tomatillos balance the chiles by adding a bright, almost citrusy, flavor. Topped with garnishes in a range of colors and textures, a bowl of this soup is an inviting meal.*

In a cumin-accented gumbo, the sweetness of a red pepper stands in for the vegetal flavor of a green pepper among the "holy trinity" of aromatic vegetables. Paprika-laced chorizo sausage adds piquancy and meaty, savory underpinnings.

# cumin-spiced shrimp and chorizo gumbo

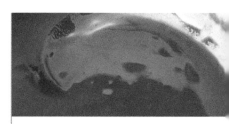

**small shell-on shrimp,**
1½ pounds

**ice cubes,** 1½ cups

**yellow onions,** 2, finely
chopped

**celery stalk,** 1, finely
chopped

**red bell pepper,** 1, seeded
and finely chopped

**garlic,** 4 cloves, minced

**ground cumin,**
1 tablespoon

**cayenne pepper,**
⅛ teaspoon

**canola oil,** ½ cup

**all-purpose flour,** ½ cup

**dried bay leaves,** 2

**spanish chorizo,** 1 pound,
cut into slices ¼ inch thick

**kosher salt and freshly
ground pepper**

**green onions,** 5, thinly
sliced

**fresh flat-leaf parsley,**
3 tablespoons minced

MAKES 6–8 SERVINGS

Peel and devein the shrimp, adding the shells to a large saucepan. Cover and refrigerate the shrimp until needed. Add 4½ cups water to the pan with the shrimp shells and bring to a boil over high heat. Reduce the heat to low and simmer, uncovered, until fragrant, about 20 minutes. Strain the shrimp stock through a fine-mesh sieve into a bowl, add the ice cubes, stir to melt the ice and cool the stock, and set aside. Discard the shrimp shells.

In a bowl, combine the onions, celery, bell pepper, garlic, cumin, and cayenne and toss to mix well.

In a large Dutch oven or other heavy pot, heat the oil over medium heat. Gradually add the flour, stirring constantly with a wooden spoon to work out any lumps. Cook, stirring constantly and taking care to reach into the corners of the pot, until the mixture, now called a roux, turns to the color of an old penny, about 20 minutes. (If the roux begins to smoke, remove the pot from the heat for a moment to let it cool slightly.)

Add the vegetable mixture to the roux and cook, stirring often, until the vegetables are softened, about 7 minutes. Add the shrimp stock in a slow, steady stream while stirring vigorously. Raise the heat to high and bring to a boil, then reduce the heat to medium-low. Add the bay leaves and simmer, skimming off any foam that rises to the surface, for 20 minutes. Add the chorizo and simmer to blend the flavors, about 20 minutes longer, continuing to skim foam as it forms on the surface. Add the shrimp and simmer until opaque throughout, about 4 minutes.

Remove from the heat and remove and discard the bay leaves. Add 1½ teaspoons salt, pepper to taste, half of the green onions, and the parsley and stir to combine. Ladle the gumbo into warmed bowls, garnish with the remaining green onions, and serve right away.

*Dark roux, a humble mixture of flour and oil cooked until it's as dark as pecans and smells like a slice of whole-wheat toast, is the traditional flavor base and thickener for gumbo. It infuses the whole pot with a deep, toasty essence, laying the foundation for the earthy cumin, spicy chorizo, and sweet shrimp that star in this dish of Southern influence.*

# spicy turkey and jasmine rice soup with lemongrass

*Lemongrass is citrusy and lightly herbal in taste, with a crisp, refreshing aroma and none of the acidity of actual lemon. The fragrant herb shines new light on a familiar turkey soup that also receives a flavor boost from ginger, garlic, hot chiles, and jasmine rice.*

Pull off and discard the dry outer layers of the lemongrass stalks. Using a chef's knife, cut off the tops of the stalks where they begin to toughen and discard them. Bruise the stalks with the flat side of the knife, and then mince them. Peel the ginger, cut it into 4 equal slices, and crush each piece with the flat side of the knife. Seed and mince 2 of the serrano chiles; cut the remaining chile crosswise into very thin rings and set aside.

In a large Dutch oven or other heavy pot, warm the oil over medium heat. Add the onion and sauté until softened, about 5 minutes. Stir in the garlic, minced chiles, and lemongrass and cook until fragrant, about 45 seconds. Raise the heat to high, add the ginger, carrots, turkey stock, and wine and bring to a boil. Stir in the rice, the shredded turkey meat, 2 teaspoons salt, and pepper to taste, reduce the heat to low, and simmer until the rice is tender, about 15 minutes. Remove and discard the ginger pieces.

Taste the soup and adjust the seasonings. Ladle the soup into warmed bowls, garnish with the reserved chile slices, and serve right away.

**fresh lemongrass,** 4 stalks

**fresh ginger,** 1-inch piece

**serrano chiles,** 3

**canola oil,** 2 teaspoons

**yellow onion,** 1, finely chopped

**garlic,** 3 cloves, minced

**carrots,** 3, peeled and thinly sliced

**turkey stock (page 143),** 8 cups, plus shredded meat reserved from making the broth

**dry white wine,** 1 cup

**uncooked jasmine rice,** ¾ cup

**kosher salt and freshly ground pepper**

MAKES 6–8 SERVINGS

# golden beet soup with dilled goat cheese cream

**golden beets,** 5 (2½ pounds total weight), greens removed

**yukon gold potato,** 1

**fresh goat cheese,** ¼ pound, crumbled

**half-and-half,** ¾ cup, plus more as needed

**fresh lemon juice,** ½ teaspoon

**fresh dill,** 3 tablespoons minced, plus leaves for garnish

**kosher salt and freshly ground pepper**

**unsalted butter,** 2 tablespoons

**yellow onion,** 1, chopped

**garlic,** 2 cloves, minced

**chicken stock (page 142) or low-sodium chicken broth,** 6 cups

**white wine vinegar,** 1 teaspoon

**sugar,** pinch (optional)

MAKES 6–8 SERVINGS

Preheat the oven to 400°F. Wrap the beets and potato together in a large sheet of aluminum foil and place on a rimmed baking sheet. Roast until the vegetables are tender when pierced with the tip of a paring knife, about 1 hour. Open the foil and let cool.

Meanwhile, in a small bowl, combine the goat cheese, ¼ cup of the half-and-half, the lemon juice, minced dill, ¼ teaspoon salt, and pepper to taste. Using a fork, vigorously beat the ingredients until blended and pourable, but thick (the texture should be similar to that of whole-milk yogurt). Adjust the consistency with half-and-half as needed.

Slip off and discard the skins from the beets and potato and chop both.

In a large Dutch oven or other heavy pot with a lid, melt the butter over medium heat. Add the onion and sauté until softened, about 5 minutes. Add the garlic and cook until fragrant, about 45 seconds. Add the stock, raise the heat to medium-high, and bring to a boil. Add the chopped beets and potato, reduce the heat to low, cover partially, and cook to blend the flavors, about 15 minutes.

Working in batches, transfer the mixture to a blender and process to a smooth purée. Pour the purée into a clean pot. Add the vinegar, 1½ teaspoons salt, pepper to taste, and the remaining ½ cup half-and-half and stir to blend. Place over medium-low heat and cook gently, stirring occasionally, until heated through, about 10 minutes.

Taste the soup and adjust the seasonings, adding the sugar, if desired. Ladle into warmed bowls, garnish each serving with a dollop of the goat cheese cream mixture and a few dill leaves, and serve right away.

*With its distinct caraway nuances and celery-like flavor, feathery dill complements both earthy beets and tangy fresh goat cheese. Golden beets are as sweet as their crimson cousins, but they have a finer, milder taste that is key to this silky soup.*

Tiny green lentils have an earthiness all their own. They take on a sweet note when first sautéed with an aromatic trio of onions, carrots, and celery. Frilly-leaved Swiss chard brings a vegetal, mineral-touched taste for a lentil soup with a breadth of flavors.

# lentil and swiss chard soup with serrano ham and smoked paprika

**french green lentils,** 1 cup

**thinly sliced serrano ham,** ¼ pound

**extra-virgin olive oil,** 3 tablespoons

**yellow onion,** 1 large, finely chopped

**carrots,** 2, peeled and finely chopped

**celery stalk,** 1, finely chopped

**garlic,** 3 cloves, minced

**smoked paprika,** 2 teaspoons

**diced tomatoes,** 1 can (14½ ounces)

**dry red wine,** ½ cup

**chicken stock (page 142) or low-sodium chicken broth,** 6 cups

**fresh thyme,** 2 sprigs

**dried bay leaf,** 1

**swiss chard,** ½ bunch

**kosher salt and freshly ground pepper**

MAKES 6–8 SERVINGS

Pick over the lentils, discarding any stones or misshapen or discolored lentils, and rinse well under running water. Cut the ham into thin ribbons.

In a large Dutch oven or other heavy pot with a lid, heat the olive oil over medium heat. Add the onion, carrots, and celery and sauté until the vegetables soften and turn golden brown, about 10 minutes. Add two-thirds of the ham, garlic, and smoked paprika and sauté until fragrant, about 1 minute. Add the tomatoes with their juices, the wine, and the lentils and cook until some of the moisture evaporates and the lentils darken a little, about 5 minutes. Add the stock, thyme sprigs, and bay leaf, raise the heat to high, and bring to a boil. Reduce the heat to low, cover partially, and simmer, stirring occasionally, until the lentils are tender, about 30 minutes. Remove and discard the thyme sprigs and bay leaf.

Cut the chard stems crosswise into 1-inch pieces and the leaves crosswise into 1-inch strips. Add the chard stems to the pot along with 1¼ teaspoons salt and pepper to taste. Raise the heat to medium and cook, stirring occasionally, until the chard stems are tender-crisp, about 5 minutes. Stir in the chard leaves, and cook until wilted and tender, about 3 minutes longer.

Taste the soup and adjust the seasonings. Ladle it into warmed bowls, garnish with the remaining ham, and serve right away.

*Serrano ham lends this rustic Spanish-influenced soup a rich, meaty flavor while smoked paprika gives it earthy backbone and a subtle smokiness. Lentils and chard add substance and texture; tomatoes and red wine bring a welcome acidity that brightens up the deep, hearty flavors of the soup.*

# miso broth with shrimp, tofu, and shiitake mushrooms

*White miso tastes salty, deep, and powerful to be sure, but it also has a hint of sweetness. In this soup, miso's savory nature underscores the meatiness of the dried shiitake mushrooms, while the paste's sweet side highlights the delicate flavor of the shrimp.*

In a bowl, soak the mushrooms in 1½ cups of hot water until softened, about 30 minutes. Lift out the mushrooms and cut off and discard the stems, then thinly slice the caps. Discard the mushroom soaking liquid. Pat the tofu dry with paper towels and cut into ½-inch cubes. Divide the sliced mushrooms and the tofu cubes evenly among 6–8 bowls.

In a saucepan, combine the *kombu* and 8 cups water and bring to a simmer over medium heat; do not let it boil. As soon as the liquid reaches a simmer, remove and discard the *kombu*. Add the bonito flakes and stir to distribute them. Remove the pan from the heat and let stand, covered, until the bonito flakes sink to the bottom and the broth is fragrant, about 5 minutes.

Strain the broth through a fine-mesh sieve into a heatproof bowl. Discard the bonito flakes. Return the broth to the saucepan and bring to a simmer over medium heat. Add the shrimp, reduce the heat to low, and simmer gently until they are opaque throughout, 3–5 minutes.

Using a slotted spoon, distribute the shrimp equally among the bowls. Transfer 1 cup of the broth to a heatproof bowl, add the miso, and whisk to combine. Pour the miso mixture back into the saucepan and stir to blend. Raise the heat to medium and bring to a simmer. Ladle the hot miso broth into the bowls, garnish with the green onions, and serve right away.

**dried shiitake mushrooms,** 12

**extra-firm or firm tofu,** 7 ounces

*kombu,* two 4-inch-square pieces

**bonito flakes,** 1½ cups lightly packed

**medium shrimp,** 1½ pounds, peeled and deveined

**white miso,** ⅔ cup

**green onions,** 4, thinly sliced

MAKES 6–8 SERVINGS

# chestnut and celery root soup with sage croutons and bacon

**good-quality french or italian bread,** ½ loaf (1-pound loaf)

**unsalted butter,** 2 tablespoons

**olive oil,** 2 tablespoons

**garlic,** 2 cloves, crushed

**fresh sage,** 4 teaspoons chopped

**kosher salt and freshly ground pepper**

**bacon,** 6 slices

**yellow onion,** 1, chopped

**celery stalks,** 3, chopped

**celery seed,** ¼ teaspoon

**chicken stock (page 142) or low-sodium chicken broth,** 6 cups

**celery root,** 1 (about 1 pound), peeled and chopped

**purchased steamed peeled chestnuts,** 1 jar (15 ounces)

**half-and-half,** ½ cup

MAKES 6–8 SERVINGS

Cut off and discard the crusts from the bread. Cut the bread into ½-inch cubes; you should have about 4 cups bread cubes.

In a large frying pan, melt 1 tablespoon of the butter with the olive oil over medium-low heat. Add the garlic and half of the sage and cook gently until the garlic is light golden brown, about 5 minutes. Remove and discard the garlic. Raise the heat to medium, add ¼ teaspoon salt and the bread cubes, and stir to coat the cubes with the flavored oil. Cook, stirring and tossing often, until the croutons are crisp and toasted, 10–12 minutes.

In a large Dutch oven or other heavy pot with a lid, cook the bacon over medium heat until crisp, about 8 minutes. Transfer to a paper towel–lined plate to drain. Pour off all but 2 tablespoons of fat from the pot and return to medium heat. Add the remaining 1 tablespoon butter, the onion, and the celery and sauté until softened, about 7 minutes. Add the celery seed and cook, stirring often, until fragrant, about 1 minute. Add the stock, raise the heat to medium-high, and bring to a boil. Add the celery root and chestnuts and return to a boil, then reduce the heat to low, cover partially, and simmer until the celery root is tender when pierced with the tip of a knife, about 25 minutes. Meanwhile, crumble the bacon and set aside.

Working in batches, transfer the mixture to a blender and process to a smooth purée. Pour the purée into a clean pot. Add the half-and-half, 1½ teaspoons salt, and pepper to taste and place over medium-low heat. Cook gently, stirring occasionally, until heated through, about 10 minutes.

Taste the soup and adjust the seasonings. Ladle into warmed bowls, garnish with the bacon, croutons, and remaining sage, and serve right away.

*Fresh sage has just a hint of bitterness and a woodsy, assertive taste. Here, it is used only in the garnishes for this luxurious fall soup. Rather than overpower, it becomes a harmonious flavor accent for the mellow sweetness of the chestnuts and celery root in the soup, and the salty bacon crumbled on top.*

In a rich, silken, Indian-inspired soup, mild-tasting cauliflower is transformed from ordinary to wonderfully exotic. Fresh ginger, bright and spicy with hints of citrus and pepper, lends the dish its allure and a warm, inviting fragrance.

# cauliflower mulligatawny

**cauliflower,** 1 head (about 2 pounds)

**granny smith apple,** 1 large

**unsalted butter,** 2 tablespoons

**yellow onions,** 2, chopped

**carrots,** 3, peeled and chopped

**garlic,** 3 cloves, minced

**fresh ginger,** 2-inch piece, peeled and minced

**curry powder,** 1½ tablespoons

**ground cumin,** 1 teaspoon

**chicken stock (page 142) or low-sodium chicken or vegetable broth,** 6 cups

**unsweetened coconut milk,** 1 can (14 ounces)

**unsweetened shredded coconut,** ½ cup, toasted (page 145)

**kosher salt and freshly ground pepper**

**fresh cilantro leaves,** ¼ cup

MAKES 6–8 SERVINGS

Remove and discard the leaves from the cauliflower and break it into bite-sized florets; set aside. Cut the apple into quarters and remove and discard the core. Chop three of the apple quarters and reserve the fourth; set aside.

In a large Dutch oven or other heavy pot with a lid, melt the butter over medium heat. Add the onions and carrots and sauté until softened, about 6 minutes. Stir in two-thirds each of the garlic and ginger and cook until fragrant, about 45 seconds. Add the curry and cumin and cook, stirring constantly, until fragrant, about 1 minute. Reduce the heat to low, cover, and cook until the vegetables have released some of their moisture and are very soft, about 7 minutes. Add the stock and coconut milk, raise the heat to high, and bring to a boil. Add the cauliflower, chopped apple, and half of the toasted coconut and return to a boil. Reduce the heat to low, cover partially, and simmer until the cauliflower is very tender, about 30 minutes.

Add the remaining minced garlic and ginger to the pot and stir to blend well. Working in batches, transfer the mixture to a blender and process to a smooth purée. Pour the purée into a clean pot, add 1½ teaspoons salt and pepper to taste, and place over medium-low heat. Cook gently, stirring occasionally, until the soup is heated through, about 10 minutes. Meanwhile, cut the reserved apple quarter into thin strips.

Taste the soup and adjust the seasonings. Ladle it into warmed bowls and garnish with the remaining coconut, the apple strips, and the cilantro leaves. Serve right away.

*Golden, pungent, and warmly spiced, curry powder adds a heady aroma and lush taste to this simple, but full-flavored, soup. The rich coconut milk and tart apple counters the curry's heat as well as the bite of ginger and garlic.*

winter

# kale and roasted sweet potato soup with lamb sausage

**sweet potatoes,** 3 (about 2 pounds total weight)

**olive oil,** 2 tablespoons

**kosher salt and freshly ground pepper**

**lamb sausage, such as** *merguez,* ½ pound

**yellow onion,** 1 large, finely chopped

**garlic,** 4 cloves, minced

**fresh thyme,** 2 teaspoons minced

**chicken stock (page 142) or low-sodium chicken broth,** 8 cups

**red potato,** 1 large, peeled and cut into ¾-inch pieces

**kale,** 1 small bunch (about 1 pound)

**fresh flat-leaf parsley,** 3 tablespoons chopped (optional)

MAKES 6–8 SERVINGS

Preheat the oven to 450°F. Line a rimmed baking sheet with aluminum foil. Cut the sweet potatoes into wedges about 1 inch thick, and then cut each wedge crosswise into pieces about 1½ inches long. In a large bowl, combine the sweet potatoes, 1½ tablespoons of the olive oil, and salt and pepper to taste and toss to coat. Spread in a single layer on the prepared baking sheet and roast until just barely tender (the tip of a paring knife meets some resistance when inserted into the pieces), about 20 minutes.

In a large Dutch oven or other heavy pot with a lid, heat the remaining ½ tablespoon olive over medium heat. Add the sausage and cook, turning occasionally, until browned all over, about 8 minutes. Transfer to a paper towel–lined plate to drain. Add the onion to the pot and sauté until softened, about 5 minutes. Stir in the garlic and thyme and cook until fragrant, about 45 seconds. Add 3 cups of the stock, raise the heat to high, and bring to a boil, using a wooden spoon to scrape up the browned bits from the bottom of the pot. Add the red potato, cover, and cook until the potato is completely tender, about 25 minutes. Meanwhile, cut the sausage into slices ½ inch thick. Trim off and discard the stems from the kale, and then cut the leaves crosswise into ¼-inch pieces.

Use a wooden spoon to mash the potato cubes against the side of the pot, then stir them into the soup until the soup thickens slightly. Add the sausage and remaining 5 cups stock and bring to a boil. Reduce the heat to low and simmer to blend the flavors, about 10 minutes. Raise the heat to medium, add 2 teaspoons salt, pepper to taste, the roasted sweet potatoes, and the kale, pushing down on the vegetables to submerge them in the liquid. Cook, stirring often, until the kale is tender, about 8 minutes.

Taste the soup and adjust the seasonings. Ladle it into warmed bowls, garnish with the parsley, if using, and serve right away.

*North African in origin, merguez sausage often contains lamb, which gives it a distinctive flavor and meatiness. Playing off its richness are hot, pungent red spices, such as paprika, cayenne, and other chiles. Here, sweet potatoes and vegetal kale are great foils for the spicy sausage.*

# pinto bean soup with toasted jalapeño chiles and garlic

*Toasting fresh chiles and garlic on the stove top until they're charred and blistered deepens and mellows their strong flavors, coaxing out a subtle sweetness and adding a suggestion of smokiness. These ingredients, along with a meaty ham hock, musky spices, and tangy lime juice, give this Mexican-style soup bold flavor.*

In a large saucepan, combine the stock and ham hock and bring to a boil over medium-high heat. Reduce the heat to low, cover, and simmer until the broth is smoky and fragrant, about 1 hour. Discard the ham hock.

In a small frying pan, combine the jalapeños and garlic cloves over medium heat. Toast, tossing occasionally, until spotty brown all over, about 15 minutes. Transfer to a cutting board and let cool. Seed and mince 4 of the chiles. Cut the remaining 2 chiles into thin rings, removing the seeds if desired; set aside the minced chiles and chile rings separately. Mince the garlic and set aside.

In a large Dutch oven or other heavy pot, warm the olive oil over medium heat. Add the onions and carrots and sauté until softened, about 6 minutes. Stir in the minced chiles, the garlic, oregano, cumin, coriander, and chili powder and cook until fragrant, about 2 minutes. Add the ham broth, the tomatoes with their juices, and the cooked beans. Raise the heat to high and bring to a boil, then reduce the heat to low and simmer to blend the flavors, about 20 minutes.

Transfer half of the mixture to a blender and process to a smooth purée. Return the purée to the pot with the unpuréed mixture. Add the lime juice, 2½ teaspoons salt, and pepper to taste, stir to mix well, and place over medium-low heat. Cook gently, stirring occasionally, until heated through, about 10 minutes.

Taste the soup and adjust the seasonings. Ladle it into warmed bowls and garnish each serving with a dollop of sour cream, a few of the roasted jalapeño rings, and a sprinkling of cilantro leaves. Serve right away.

**chicken stock (page 142) or low-sodium chicken broth,** 6 cups

**smoked ham hock,** 1

**jalapeño chiles,** 6

**garlic,** 4 cloves, peeled

**olive oil,** 2 tablespoons

**yellow onions,** 2, finely chopped

**carrots,** 2, peeled and finely chopped

**dried oregano and ground cumin,** 1½ teaspoons *each*

**ground coriander and chili powder,** ¾ teaspoon *each*

**diced tomatoes,** 1 can (14½ ounces)

**dried pinto beans,** ¾ pound, cooked and drained (page 145)

**fresh lime juice,** ¼ cup

**kosher salt and freshly ground pepper**

**sour cream,** 1 cup

**fresh cilantro leaves,** ⅓ cup

MAKES 6–8 SERVINGS

Traditional English Cheddar is the star ingredient in an unusual soup that features a delicious pairing of fruit and cheese. Cheddar's rich and rugged flavor is balanced by crisp, fruity hard apple cider. A scattering of golden fried shallot rings make the soup even more memorable.

# cheddar and hard cider soup with fried shallots

*Bay leaves are remarkable for their ability to infuse foods with a savory, multi-layered fragrance that hints at pepper, pine, cinnamon, and even flowers. Their subtleties may be elusive, but in this velvety soup, bay leaves add a fullness and range of flavor that ties together all the elements.*

In a large Dutch oven or other heavy pot with a lid, melt 3 tablespoons of the butter over medium-high heat. Add the onions, celery, potato, and garlic and stir to mix well. Reduce the heat to low, cover, and cook, stirring occasionally, until the vegetables are softened, about 12 minutes. Sprinkle the flour over the vegetables and cook, stirring constantly, until the flour is incorporated. While stirring constantly, gradually add the stock, cider, and half-and-half. Raise the heat to medium-high, add the bay leaves and thyme sprigs, and bring to a boil. Reduce the heat to low and simmer to blend the flavors, about 10 minutes.

Meanwhile, in a small frying pan, melt the remaining 1 tablespoon butter with the oil over medium-high heat. Add the shallots and ¼ teaspoon salt and cook, stirring often, until the shallots are deep golden brown, about 8 minutes. Using a slotted spoon, transfer the shallots to a paper towel–lined plate to drain.

Remove and discard the bay leaves and thyme sprigs from the soup base. Working in batches, transfer the soup base to a blender and process to a smooth purée. Pour the purée into a clean pot. Stir in the applejack. Off the heat, while whisking constantly, gradually add the cheese one handful at a time. Continue whisking until all the cheese is melted. Place over medium-low heat, stir in 1 teaspoon salt and pepper to taste, and cook gently, stirring often, until heated through, about 10 minutes.

Taste the soup and adjust the seasonings. Ladle it into warmed bowls, garnish with the fried shallots, and serve right away.

**unsalted butter,** 4 tablespoons

**yellow onions,** 2, chopped

**celery stalk,** 1, chopped

**yukon gold potato,** 1, peeled and chopped

**garlic,** 2 cloves, minced

**all-purpose flour,** 2 tablespoons

**chicken stock (page 142) or low-sodium chicken broth,** 2½ cups

**hard apple cider,** 2½ cups

**half-and-half,** 1 cup

**dried bay leaves,** 2

**fresh thyme,** 2 sprigs

**canola oil,** 1 tablespoon

**shallots,** 3, thinly sliced

**kosher salt and freshly ground pepper**

**applejack or calvados,** 2 tablespoons

**english cheddar cheese,** ¾ pound, shredded

MAKES 6–8 SERVINGS

# napa cabbage soup with pork, mushrooms, and bean sprouts

fresh ginger, 4-inch piece

chicken stock (page 142) or low-sodium chicken broth, 6 cups

chinese rice wine or dry sherry, ½ cup, plus 3 tablespoons

soy sauce, 5 tablespoons

boneless pork loin chop, ½ pound, cut into thin strips

dried shiitake mushrooms, 10

napa cabbage, 1 head (about 2½ pounds)

canola oil, 4 teaspoons

garlic, 6 cloves, minced

asian sesame oil, 2 teaspoons

kosher salt

fresh mung bean sprouts, 1½ cups

asian chili oil for serving

green onions, 6, green tops thinly sliced

MAKES 6–8 SERVINGS

Peel the ginger, mince half of it, and set it aside. Cut the other half into 6 equal slices and crush each slice with the flat side of a chef's knife. In a large saucepan, combine the crushed ginger, the stock, and the ½ cup rice wine and bring to a boil over high heat. Remove from the heat, cover, and let stand to blend the flavors, about 30 minutes. Using a slotted spoon, remove and discard the crushed ginger.

In a small bowl, stir together the minced ginger, the 3 tablespoons rice wine, 2 tablespoons of the soy sauce, and the thin strips of pork. Let stand at room temperature for 30 minutes. Meanwhile, in a bowl, soak the mushrooms in 1 cup of hot water until softened, about 30 minutes. Lift out the mushrooms and cut off and discard the stems, then cut the caps into quarters and set aside. Pour the soaking liquid through a fine-mesh sieve lined with damp cheesecloth into the saucepan. Separate the leaf layers from the head of cabbage and cut the leaves crosswise into 1-inch pieces.

In a large nonstick frying pan, warm 2 teaspoons of the canola oil over high heat. Add the cabbage pieces and stir-fry for 1 minute. Add the garlic and stir-fry until the cabbage is just tender-crisp, about 2 minutes longer, then scrape into the pot with the broth. Add the remaining 2 teaspoons canola oil to the frying pan and warm over high heat. Add the mushrooms and the pork with its marinade and stir-fry until the pork is opaque, about 2 minutes; scrape into the pot with the broth. Add the remaining 3 tablespoons soy sauce to the broth along with the sesame oil and 1 teaspoon salt. Bring to a boil over high heat, reduce the heat to low, cover partially, and simmer to blend the flavors, 10–15 minutes.

Taste the soup and adjust the seasoning. Ladle it into warmed bowls, then garnish each serving with about ¼ cup of the bean sprouts, a drizzle of chili oil, and a sprinkling of the green onion tops. Serve right away.

*Once rehydrated, dried shiitake mushrooms assume a chewy, almost meaty, texture, and their soaking water is infused with woodsy, smoky flavor. This liquid, used as an ingredient as it is here, lends a dish even more of the mushrooms' earthiness. The broth is a savory background for mild-tasting cabbage, hot chili oil, and the snap of fresh bean sprouts.*

There is a taste of the sea in both the flaky meat and the spiny shells of king crab legs. They each are used to a delicious effect in a refined bisque, one that brings together crab's gentle sweetness with caramelized roasted shallots.

# roasted shallot and crab bisque with sherry

**shallots,** 1 pound, peeled

**olive oil,** 2 tablespoons

**canned diced tomatoes with juices,** ¾ cup

**cayenne pepper,** pinch

**white rice,** ⅓ cup

**crab stock (page 143),** 4 cups, plus shredded crabmeat from making stock

**dry white wine,** ½ cup

**dry sherry,** ⅓ cup

**half-and-half,** 1 cup

**fresh lemon juice,** 1 tablespoon

**kosher salt and freshly ground white pepper**

**fresh chives,** ¼ cup snipped

MAKES 6–8 SERVINGS

Preheat the oven to 400°F. In a bowl, toss the shallots with 1 tablespoon of the olive oil. Spread in a single layer on a rimmed baking sheet and roast for 20 minutes. Stir the shallots and continue roasting until browned and tender, about 20 minutes longer.

In a large saucepan, warm the remaining 1 tablespoon olive oil over medium heat. Add two-thirds of the roasted shallots, the tomatoes, the cayenne, and the rice and stir to mix well. Add the crab stock and white wine, raise the heat to high, and bring to a boil. Reduce the heat to low, cover, and simmer until the rice is completely tender, about 30 minutes. Meanwhile, finely chop the remaining roasted shallots and set aside.

Working in batches, transfer the soup base to a blender and process to a smooth purée. Pour the purée into a clean pot. Add the chopped roasted shallots, the crabmeat, sherry, half-and-half, lemon juice, 2¼ teaspoons salt, and white pepper to taste. Place over medium-low heat and cook gently, stirring occasionally, until heated through, about 10 minutes.

Taste the bisque and adjust the seasonings. Ladle it into warmed bowls, garnish with the chives, and serve right away.

*Dry sherry, the iconic wine of Spain, hits a wide range of flavor nuances, including oaky, nutty, caramelized, and crisp. In this satiny bisque, dry sherry provides elegant underpinnings for the sweet roasted shallots and delicate, briny crab.*

# baby bok choy and beef noodle soup with warm spices

*Peppery, piquant, and with a slight lemony edge, fresh ginger invigorates any dish to which it is added. This simple meal-in-a-bowl gets its warm flavor from ginger, as well as from cinnamon and star anise. Garlic and chile paste lend pungency; chewy noodles and tender slices of beef add heartiness.*

Peel the ginger, cut it into thin slices, and crush each slice with the flat side of a chef's knife.

In a large Dutch oven or other heavy pot with a lid, warm the oil over medium-high heat. Add the onion and sauté until softened, about 3 minutes. Add the cinnamon sticks and star anise and cook, stirring constantly, until fragrant and the cinnamon sticks begin to uncurl, about 2 minutes. Add the crushed ginger, garlic, and chile paste and cook, stirring constantly, until fragrant, about 45 seconds. Add the stock, soy sauce, and 4½ cups water. Raise the heat to high, cover, and bring to a boil. Stir in the sliced beef and return to a boil. Reduce the heat to low, cover partially, and simmer until the beef is very tender, about 1½ hours.

Meanwhile, trim the bottom ends of the bok choy and cut each head lengthwise into quarters.

In a large saucepan, bring 4 quarts water to a boil over high heat. Stir in 1 tablespoon salt and the noodles, return to a boil, and cook until the noodles are tender, about 3 minutes. Drain the noodles, rinse well under warm running water, and drain well again. Divide the noodles evenly among 6–8 warmed bowls.

Using a slotted spoon, remove and discard the cinnamon sticks, star anise, and ginger from the broth. Add the bok choy and cook just until tender-crisp, about 5 minutes. Add half of the green onions and stir to combine.

Taste the soup and adjust the seasoning. Ladle it over the noodles, distributing the beef and bok choy equally. Garnish with the remaining green onions and serve right away.

**fresh ginger,** 4-inch piece

**canola oil,** 2 tablespoons

**yellow onion,** 1, thinly sliced

**cinnamon sticks,** 4

**whole star anise,** 1

**garlic,** 5 cloves, crushed and thinly sliced

**asian chile garlic paste,** 2 teaspoons

**chicken stock (page 142) or low-sodium chicken broth,** 4 cups

**soy sauce,** ½ cup

**beef blade steak,** 2 pounds, trimmed and cut into slices ¼ inch thick

**baby bok choy,** 5 (about 1½ pounds total weight)

**kosher salt**

**fresh chinese wheat noodles,** 1½ pounds

**green onions,** 4, thinly sliced

MAKES 6–8 SERVINGS

# moroccan-spiced lamb and chickpea soup

**lamb leg steak or boneless lamb shoulder,** 1½ pounds

**olive oil for browning**

**yellow onions,** 2, finely chopped

**carrots,** 3, peeled and cut into rounds ¼ inch thick

**garlic,** 3 cloves, minced

**cinnamon sticks,** 2

**sweet paprika,** ¾ teaspoon

**ground cumin,** ½ teaspoon

**cayenne pepper**

**chicken stock (page 142) or low-sodium chicken broth,** 6 cups

**kosher salt and freshly ground pepper**

**chickpeas,** 1 can (29 ounces)

**diced tomatoes,** 1 can (28 ounces)

**zucchini,** 2 small

**fresh cilantro,** 1 bunch

**lemon,** ½

MAKES 6–8 SERVINGS

Trim the lamb of excess fat and cut into 1-inch chunks. In a large Dutch oven or other heavy pot, warm 2 teaspoons olive oil over medium-high heat. Working in batches to avoid overcrowding, brown the lamb on all sides, about 5 minutes per batch; transfer the browned meat to a large bowl. Add more olive oil to the pot as needed.

When all of the meat is browned, add 2 teaspoons olive oil, the onions, and carrots to the pot. Reduce the heat to medium and sauté until the vegetables are softened, about 6 minutes. Stir in the garlic, cinnamon sticks, paprika, cumin, and a large pinch of cayenne and cook, stirring often, until fragrant, about 1 minute.

Add the stock, raise the heat to high, and use a wooden spoon to scrape up the browned bits from the bottom of the pot. Return the browned lamb and any accumulated juices to the pot. Stir in 1 teaspoon salt and 1 teaspoon pepper and bring to a boil, then reduce the heat to low and simmer until the meat is just starting to become tender, about 30 minutes.

Rinse the chickpeas and drain well. Add the chickpeas and the tomatoes with their juices to the pot and continue simmering until the lamb is completely tender, about 25 minutes.

Meanwhile, cut the zucchini in half lengthwise, and then cut each half crosswise into pieces ½ inch thick. Chop enough of the cilantro leaves to measure ½ cup. Squeeze the lemon half and measure 2 tablespoons lemon juice. Add the zucchini and half of the cilantro to the pot, stir to mix, and cook until the zucchini is tender, about 4 minutes. Stir in the lemon juice, then remove and discard the cinnamon sticks.

Taste the soup and adjust the seasonings. Ladle it into warmed bowls, garnish with the remaining cilantro, and serve right away.

*Warm, sweet, aromatic cinnamon is not exclusive to desserts. Here, the warming spice combines with garlic, cumin, paprika, and cayenne to season a dish of rich flavors, colors, and textures that captures the spirit of exotic Moroccan cuisine.*

Deeply browning chicken thighs develops a solid foundation of flavor for a hearty soup redolent with earthy, smoky dried chiles. Fresh cilantro and all of its citrusy, herbal nuances add a bright counterpoint to the soup's intensity.

# chicken and hominy soup with ancho chiles

**ancho chiles**, 4 large, stemmed and seeded, flesh torn into pieces

**boiling water**, 1⅔ cups

**bone-in, skin-on chicken thighs**, 3 pounds

**kosher salt and freshly ground pepper**

**canola oil for browning**

**yellow onions**, 2, finely chopped

**garlic**, 4 cloves, minced

**ground cumin**, 1 tablespoon

**fresh oregano**, 1 tablespoon minced

**chicken stock (page 142) or low-sodium chicken broth**, 6 cups

**diced tomatoes**, 1 can (14½ ounces)

**hominy**, 2 cans (29 ounces each), rinsed and drained

**fresh cilantro leaves**, ¼ cup

**lime**, 1, cut into wedges

MAKES 6–8 SERVINGS

In a heatproof bowl, soak the chiles in the boiling water until softened, about 25 minutes. Transfer the chiles and their soaking liquid to a blender and process to a purée. Strain the purée though a fine-mesh sieve, pressing on the solids to extract as much liquid as possible. Discard the solids.

Season the chicken generously with salt and pepper. In a large Dutch oven or other heavy pot with a lid, warm 2 teaspoons of the oil over medium-high heat. Working in batches to avoid overcrowding, place the chicken, skin side down, in the pot and cook until golden brown, about 5 minutes. Turn the chicken pieces and cook until golden brown on the second sides, about 5 minutes longer. Transfer the chicken to a large plate. Repeat to brown the remaining chicken pieces, adding more oil to the pot if needed. Remove and discard the skin from the browned chicken.

Pour off all but 1 tablespoon of fat from the pot and place over medium heat. Add about three-fourths of the chopped onions and sauté until softened, about 5 minutes. Stir in the garlic, cumin, and oregano and cook until fragrant, about 45 seconds. Raise the heat to high, add the stock, and using a wooden spoon, scrape up the browned bits from the bottom of the pot. Add the chicken and any accumulated juices, the tomatoes with their juices, and 1½ teaspoons salt and bring to a boil. Reduce the heat to low, cover partially, and simmer until the chicken is tender, about 40 minutes.

Transfer the chicken to a bowl. When cool enough to handle, shred the meat and discard the bones. Stir the shredded chicken, hominy, and chile purée into the pot. Simmer to blend the flavors, about 15 minutes.

Taste the soup and adjust the seasonings, then stir in the cilantro. Ladle the soup into warmed bowls and garnish each serving with a sprinkling of the remaining chopped onion and a lime wedge. Serve right away.

*Ancho chiles have very little heat, but they are rich with flavor—raisins, leather, tobacco, and even cocoa characterize their amazing complexity. Complemented by cumin and oregano, anchos give this hearty soup—a twist on traditional Mexican posole—lusciousness and depth. Mild-tasting hominy balances the robust flavors, and cilantro and lime are sprightly finishing touches.*

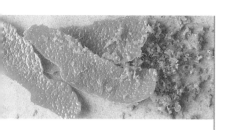

# beef stew with orange zest and black olives

*The true essence of an orange resides not in its juice, but in the oils found in the fruit's skin, or zest. Strips of orange zest, as well as finely grated zest, infuse their floral fragrance and a sunny, citrusy tang into this Provence-inspired braise, bringing balance to the richness of beef and the brininess of olives.*

Trim the beef of excess fat and cut the meat into 1½-inch chunks. In a bowl, stir together the flour, 2 teaspoons salt, and 1 teaspoon pepper. Add the beef and toss to coat. In a large Dutch oven or other heavy pot with a lid, warm 1 tablespoon of the olive oil over medium-high heat. Add half of the beef pieces, arranging them in a single layer. Cook, without stirring, until deeply browned, about 4 minutes. Turn the beef pieces and cook, again without stirring, until deeply browned on the second sides, about 4 minutes longer. Transfer to a bowl. Add 1 tablespoon olive oil to the pot and repeat to brown the remaining beef. Wipe the pot clean and set aside.

Using a vegetable peeler, remove the zest from half of the orange in wide strips. Finely grate the zest from the remaining orange half. Set aside the zest strips and grated zest separately.

Add the remaining 1 tablespoon olive oil to the pot and warm over medium heat. Add the onions and sauté until just starting to soften, about 2 minutes. Stir in the garlic, orange zest strips, thyme, and fennel seeds and sauté until fragrant, about 45 seconds. Add the wine, raise the heat to high, and bring to a boil, using a wooden spoon to scrape up the browned bits from the bottom of the pot. Cook until reduced by half, about 4 minutes. Stir in the stock and tomatoes, then add the browned beef and any accumulated juices. Bring to a boil, then reduce the heat to low, cover, and simmer until the beef is tender, about 2½ hours.

Add the carrots and olives to the pot, pushing them down into the liquid. Raise the heat to medium, cover, and cook until the carrots are tender, about 8 minutes. Stir in the grated orange zest and the parsley.

Taste the stew and adjust the seasonings. Spoon it into warmed bowls and serve right away.

**beef chuck roast,** 3 pounds

**all-purpose flour,** 2 tablespoons

**kosher salt and freshly ground pepper**

**olive oil,** 3 tablespoons

**orange,** 1

**yellow onions,** 2, chopped

**garlic,** 3 cloves, minced

**fresh thyme,** 2 teaspoons minced

**fennel seeds,** 1½ tablespoons, crushed

**dry red wine,** ¾ cup

**chicken stock (page 142) or low-sodium chicken broth,** ¾ cup

**canned diced tomatoes with juices,** 1 cup

**carrots,** 4, peeled and cut into rounds ¼ inch thick

**kalamata olives,** 1½ cups, pitted and halved

**fresh flat-leaf parsley,** ¼ cup finely chopped

MAKES 6–8 SERVINGS

# split pea soup with smoked turkey and balsamic drizzle

smoked turkey drumstick,
1 (about ¾ pound)

chicken stock (page 142)
or low-sodium chicken
broth, 8 cups

dried bay leaves, 3

dried split peas, 1 pound

fresh thyme, 1½ teaspoons
minced

red potatoes, 3 (about
1½ pounds total weight),
cut into ½-inch cubes

unsalted butter,
1 tablespoon

canola oil, 1 tablespoon

yellow onion, 1 large, finely
chopped

carrots, 3, peeled and
finely chopped

celery stalks, 2, finely
chopped

kosher salt and freshly
ground pepper

balsamic vinegar, ¾ cup

MAKES 6–8 SERVINGS

In a large Dutch oven or other heavy pot with a lid, combine the turkey drumstick, stock, and bay leaves and bring to a boil over medium-high heat. Reduce the heat to low, cover, and simmer until the broth is smoky and flavorful, about 1 hour. Remove 1 cup of broth from the pot and set aside; transfer the turkey to a plate and let cool. When the turkey is cool enough to handle, shred the meat into bite-sized pieces and set aside. Discard the skin and bone. Remove and discard the bay leaves from the broth.

Pick over the split peas, discarding any stones or misshapen or discolored peas, and rinse well under running water. Add the split peas and thyme to the broth, cover, and bring to a boil over high heat. Reduce the heat to medium and simmer until the split peas are just beginning to soften, about 15 minutes. Add the potatoes and continue simmering until both the split peas and the potatoes are completely tender, about 15 minutes longer.

Meanwhile, in a large frying pan, melt the butter with the oil over medium-high heat. Add the onion, carrots, and celery and sauté until the vegetables are browned, about 12 minutes. Add the vegetables and shredded turkey meat to the pot and simmer, stirring occasionally, until some of the split peas break down and begin to thicken the soup, about 15 minutes longer. Stir in ½ teaspoon salt and pepper to taste.

While the soup is simmering, in a small, nonreactive saucepan, bring the balsamic vinegar to a simmer over medium-high heat. Cook until syrupy and reduced by about half, about 8 minutes.

If the soup seems too thick, adjust the consistency as desired with the reserved 1 cup broth. Taste the soup and adjust the seasonings. Ladle it into warmed bowls and garnish each serving with a drizzle of the balsamic syrup. Serve right away.

*Balsamic vinegar's sweet-tart dynamic intensifies when the vinegar is cooked down to a dark, glossy syrup. A drizzle of balsamic syrup captures the palate with the way it deliciously offsets the earthy taste of humble, smoky split pea soup.*

Golden brown roasted pears, dusted with woodsy, piney rosemary are savory and sweet all at once. They're a buttery garnish for a satiny, mildy sweet butternut squash soup—it's surprising how the flavors flatter one another.

# butternut squash soup with roasted pears and rosemary

**butternut squash,** 1 (about 3 pounds)

**unsalted butter,** 2 tablespoons

**canola oil,** 1 tablespoon

**yellow onion,** 1, finely chopped

**chicken stock (page 142) or low-sodium chicken or vegetable broth,** 6 cups

**fresh rosemary,** 1 sprig, plus 1 teaspoon minced

**ripe but firm anjou or bartlett pears,** 3 large

**light brown sugar,** 4 teaspoons firmly packed

**half-and-half,** ½ cup

**kosher salt and freshly ground pepper**

MAKES 6–8 SERVINGS

Peel the squash, cut it in half lengthwise, and scoop out the seeds. Cut each half crosswise into slices ¼ inch thick.

In a large Dutch oven or other heavy pot with a lid, melt 1 tablespoon of the butter with the oil over medium heat. Add the onion and sauté until softened and beginning to brown, about 7 minutes. Add the squash slices, stock, and rosemary sprig to the pot. Raise the heat to high and bring to a boil, then reduce the heat to medium-low, cover partially, and simmer until the squash is tender, about 20 minutes.

Meanwhile, preheat the oven to 500°F. Melt the remaining 1 tablespoon butter. Peel the pears, cut them in half lengthwise, and cut out the cores. Cut each half lengthwise into slices ¼ inch thick. In a bowl, stir together the melted butter and 2 teaspoons of the brown sugar. Add the pear slices and toss to coat. Spread in a single layer on a rimmed baking sheet and roast until the bottoms begin to brown, about 8 minutes. Gently turn the pear slices over, sprinkle with the minced rosemary, and continue roasting until tender and brown, about 7 minutes longer. Using a spatula, carefully transfer to a plate and let cool. Cut half of the slices into ½-inch cubes.

Remove and discard the rosemary sprig from the pot. Working in batches, transfer the soup base to a blender and process to a smooth purée. Pour the purée into a clean pot. Add the remaining 2 teaspoons brown sugar, the half-and-half, 2½ teaspoons salt, and pepper to taste and stir to mix. Place over medium-low heat and cook gently, stirring occasionally, until heated through, about 10 minutes.

Taste the soup and adjust the seasonings. Ladle it into warmed bowls, place some diced pear into the center of each serving, and lay a few pear slices on top so they appear to float on the surface. Serve right away.

*Piney, floral, and just a bit peppery, fresh rosemary is a flavorful herbal counterpoint to all the elements of this soup—not just the sweet pears, but also the lush, velvety butternut squash, sweet onions, and rich butter and cream that are puréed to a silky finish.*

# fundamentals

*The following pages offer recipes for stocks and broths, some of which are basics that make good additions to your repertory and some that are tailored to the soups in this book. You will also find recipes for versatile soup garnishes and a handful of tips and techniques for working with many of the ingredients called for in the recipes.*

## chicken stock

6 pounds chicken necks and backs

2 yellow onions, cut into quarters

1 large carrot, peeled and coarsely chopped

1 large celery stalk, coarsely chopped

1 clove garlic

4 sprigs fresh flat-leaf parsley

1 dried bay leaf

2 teaspoons black peppercorns

In a large stockpot, combine the chicken, onions, carrot, celery, garlic, parsley, bay leaf, and peppercorns. Add water to cover the ingredients by 1 inch and bring to a boil over medium-high heat.

As soon as the liquid reaches a boil, reduce the heat to medium-low so that only small bubbles break on the surface. Skim off any foam that rises to the surface. Simmer gently for 2–2½ hours, continuing to skim foam as needed. Add more water, if necessary, to keep the ingredients just covered.

Strain the stock through a fine-mesh sieve into a large heatproof bowl, pressing on the solids to extract as much liquid as possible. Discard the solids. If using the stock right away, spoon off as much fat as possible. Or, let cool completely, cover, and refrigerate for up to 3 days; before use, lift the congealed layer of fat off the surface and discard. Makes about 4 quarts.

## fish broth

3 pounds mahi mahi or other white fish frames (bones), rinsed and broken into 3-inch pieces

½ cup dry vermouth

1 yellow onion, coarsely chopped

⅔ cup chopped fennel fronds

6 sprigs fresh thyme

2 dried bay leaves

1 teaspoon kosher salt

1 tablespoon black peppercorns

In a large stockpot, combine the fish bones and vermouth. Add just enough water to cover the bones and bring to a boil over medium-high heat. Skim off any foam that rises to the surface. Add the onion, fennel fronds, thyme, bay leaves, salt, and peppercorns, and return to a boil, continuing to skim foam as needed. Reduce the heat to low and simmer, uncovered, until the broth is rich and fragrant, about 30 minutes. Strain the broth through a fine-mesh sieve into a large heatproof bowl, pressing on the solids to extract as much liquid as possible. Discard the solids. Use the broth right away or let cool, cover, and refrigerate for up to 2 days. Makes about 5 cups.

## rich beef stock

1½–2 tablespoons olive oil, or as needed

5 pounds meaty beef shanks

1 yellow onion, quartered

3 cloves garlic, minced

⅔ cup dry red wine

3 quarts boiling water

4 sprigs fresh thyme

15 sprigs fresh flat-leaf parsley

1 tablespoon black peppercorns

In a large Dutch oven or other heavy pot with a lid, heat 1 tablespoon olive oil over medium-high heat. Working in batches, brown the beef shanks on all sides, about 12 minutes per batch; transfer the browned meat to a large bowl. Add more olive oil to the pot as needed. When all of the meat has been browned, reduce the heat to medium, heat ½ tablespoon olive oil, add the onion and garlic, and sauté until the onion begins to soften, about 2 minutes. Add the wine, raise the heat to high, and bring to a boil. Using a wooden spoon, scrape up the browned bits from the bottom of the pot. Boil until reduced to a syrup, about 2 minutes.

Return the browned meat and any accumulated juices to the pot, reduce the heat to low, cover, and cook until the meat releases its juices, about 20 minutes. Raise the heat to high and add the boiling water, thyme, parsley, and peppercorns. Bring to a boil, skimming off any foam that rises to the surface. Reduce the heat to low and simmer, continuing to skim foam as needed, until the meat is tender and the broth is flavorful, about 2½ hours.

If you're using the meat in a soup, transfer the beef to a large plate and let cool. Strain the broth through a fine-mesh sieve into a large heatproof bowl, pressing on the solids to extract as much liquid as possible. Discard the solids. Remove the meat from the bones (discard the bones), shred or cut it into ½-inch dice, and refrigerate until needed. If using the stock right away, spoon off as much fat as possible. Or, let cool completely, then cover and refrigerate overnight; before use, lift the congealed layer of fat off the surface and discard. Makes about 2 quarts.

## turkey stock

**2 large turkey wings (about 3½ pounds total weight) or 1 meaty turkey carcass**

**1 tablespoon canola oil**

**1 yellow onion, coarsely chopped**

**2½ quarts boiling water**

**2 dried bay leaves**

Using a chef's knife, cut each turkey wing at the joints into 3 pieces or cut the turkey carcass into 4- to 6-inch pieces.

In a large Dutch oven or other heavy pot with a lid, warm the oil over medium heat. Add the onion and sauté until slightly softened, about 3 minutes. Transfer the onion to a bowl and set aside. Add half of the turkey pieces to the pot and cook, turning once or twice, until golden brown all sides, about 4 minutes per side. Transfer the browned turkey to the bowl with the onion and cook the remaining turkey pieces in the same manner.

Return the onion and first batch of turkey pieces to the pot. Reduce the heat to low, cover, and cook until the turkey releases its juices, about 20 minutes. Raise the heat to high, add the boiling water and bay leaves, and skim off any foam that rises to the surface. Reduce the heat to low and simmer, uncovered, until the stock is rich and fragrant, about 2 hours.

If you're using the meat in a soup, transfer the turkey parts to a large plate and let cool.

Strain the stock through a fine-mesh sieve into a large heatproof bowl. Discard the solids in the sieve. Remove the meat from the bones (discard the bones), shred it into bite-sized pieces, and refrigerate until needed. If using the stock right away, spoon off as much fat as possible. Or, let cool completely, cover and refrigerate overnight; before use, lift the congealed layer of fat off the surface and discard. Makes about 8 cups.

## crab stock

**1 pound cooked king crab legs**

**1 tablespoon olive oil**

**1 yellow onion, finely chopped**

**1 carrot, peeled and finely chopped**

**1 celery stalk, finely chopped**

**2 cloves garlic, minced**

**⅓ cup brandy or cognac**

**¾ cup canned diced tomatoes with juices**

**½ cup dry white wine**

Pick the crabmeat out of the shells. Using your fingers, shred the crabmeat, removing any bits of shell or cartilage. Cover the crabmeat and refrigerate until needed. Using kitchen scissors, cut the shells into 1½-inch pieces and place in a brown paper bag. Using a rolling pin, gently crush the shells.

In a large Dutch oven or other heavy pot with a lid, heat the olive oil over medium-high heat. Add the onion, carrot, celery, and garlic and sauté until the vegetables are softened, about 5 minutes. Add the crab shells and cook, stirring occasionally, for 2 minutes. Add the brandy and let warm for about 10 seconds. Using a long-handled match, carefully light the brandy. Let the flames burn for 30 seconds, then cover to extinguish the flames. Add the tomatoes, wine, and 4½ cups water. Raise the heat to high and bring to a boil, then reduce the heat to low, cover partially, and simmer until flavorful, about 40 minutes, skimming off any foam that rises to the surface.

Strain the stock through a fine-mesh sieve into a large, heatproof bowl, pressing on the solids to extract as much liquid as possible. Discard the solids. Makes about 4 cups.

## lemon aioli

1 large egg yolk

2 cloves garlic, finely minced

1½ teaspoons finely grated lemon zest

1 tablespoon fresh lemon juice

½ teaspoon dijon mustard

¾ teaspoon kosher salt

¾ cup plus 2 tablespoons olive oil

In a nonreactive bowl, whisk together the egg yolk, garlic, lemon zest and juice, mustard, and salt. Whisking constantly, very slowly drizzle the olive oil into the egg-yolk mixture until it begins to thicken. As it thickens,

increase the flow of olive oil to a trickle, still whisking constantly, until all of the oil is incorporated and the sauce has thickened to the consistency of mayonnaise. If it seems too thick, whisk in water, 1 teaspoon at a time, to loosen to the desired consistency. Cover with plastic wrap and refrigerate until needed. Makes about 1 cup.

## arugula pesto

⅓ cup walnuts

2 cups baby arugula, lightly packed

1 clove garlic, minced

4 tablespoons extra-virgin olive oil

kosher salt and freshly ground pepper

Place the walnuts in a small frying pan and toast over medium heat, stirring often, until fragrant and lightly browned, 3–5 minutes. Transfer to a plate and let cool.

In a food processor, combine the walnuts, arugula, garlic, and 1 tablespoon olive oil and process to a purée, stopping to scrape down the sides of the bowl as needed. With the motor running, slowly pour in the remaining 3 tablespoons olive oil through the feed tube and process until a smooth sauce forms. Add ½ teaspoon salt and pepper to taste and pulse to combine.

Transfer the pesto to a small bowl, press plastic wrap directly onto the surface, and refrigerate until needed. Makes about ⅔ cup.

## toasted garlic croutons

3 tablespoons olive oil

2 cloves garlic, crushed

½ loaf good-quality french or italian bread, cut into ½-inch cubes (about 4 cups)

In a large frying pan, heat the olive oil over medium-low heat. Add the garlic cloves and cook gently until light golden brown, about 5 minutes. Raise the heat to medium, add the bread cubes, and stir to coat well. Cook, stirring often, until the croutons are crisp, 10–12 minutes. Makes about 4 cups.

## asiago wafers

½ teaspoon olive oil

½ pound asiago cheese, coarsely grated

Brush a large, heavy nonstick frying pan with the olive oil and heat over medium heat. Sprinkle 2 tablespoons of the cheese into the pan, making a circle about 2½ inches in diameter. Repeat to make 3 or 4 more rounds, leaving about 2 inches between them.

Cook the cheese, without disturbing it, until it melts, bubbles, spreads slightly, and begins to brown very lightly around the edges, about 3 minutes. Using a spatula, carefully loosen and turn the wafers and cook until very pale gold on the second side, about 1 minute longer. Adjust the heat as needed.

Transfer the wafers to a paper towel–lined plate. Repeat with the remaining cheese;

additional oil will not be necessary after the first batch. Let the wafers cool to room temperature. Makes about 18 wafers.

## cooking quinoa

*1 Rinse the quinoa* Place ¾ cup quinoa in a fine-mesh strainer, rinse well under cold running water, and then drain.

*2 Simmer* In a saucepan, bring 1⅓ cups water to a boil over medium-high heat. Stir in ½ teaspoon salt and the quinoa and return to a boil. Reduce the heat to low, cover, and simmer until the quinoa is plump and just tender, about 12 minutes.

*3 Let stand* Remove the saucepan from the heat and let stand, covered, until the quinoa has absorbed all of the liquid, about 12 minutes longer.

## toasting nuts and seeds

**in the oven** Scatter the nuts or seeds in an even layer in a baking dish or on a rimmed baking sheet. Toast in a 325°F or 350°F oven, stirring once or twice, until fragrant and slightly darkened in color, 5–10 minutes, depending on the size and quantity of the nuts or seeds. Let cool completely before use.

**on the stove top** Place the nuts or seeds in an even layer in a frying pan. Toast over medium heat, stirring or shaking the pan often, until fragrant and slightly darkened

in color, 2–5 minutes, depending on the size and quantity of the nuts or seeds. Let cool completely before use.

## preparing a grill for direct-heat cooking

**charcoal grill** Ignite about 2½ pounds of coals and let burn until covered with a thin coating of white ash. Spread the coals in an even layer on the fire bed and let burn until medium-hot, 20–30 minutes. Replace the grill grate and brush it lightly with oil to prevent food from sticking.

**gas grill** Turn all the burners to high heat. Close the cover and preheat the grill for 10–20 minutes. Reduce the burner settings to medium-high. Lightly brush the grill grate with oil to prevent food from sticking.

## cooking live lobsters

*1 Bring water to a boil* Bring a very large stockpot two-thirds full of lightly salted water to a rolling boil over high heat.

*2 Add the lobsters* Add the lobsters headfirst to the pot; add only as many lobsters as will comfortably fit and cook in as many batches as needed. Cover the pot and bring the liquid back to a rolling boil. Cook for 6–8 minutes until the lobsters are deep red in color.

*3 Let cool* Using tongs, transfer the lobsters to a large bowl or platter and let cool.

## cooking dried beans

*1 Pick over and rinse the beans* Pick over the beans, discarding any grit, stones, and discolored or misshapen beans. Place the beans in a sieve or colander, rinse under running water, and drain well.

*2 Bring to a boil and let stand* Place the beans in a large saucepan and add water to cover by 2 inches. Bring to a boil over high heat and let boil for 2 minutes. Remove from the heat, cover, and let stand at room temperature for 2 hours.

*3 Simmer until tender* Again add enough water to cover the beans by 2 inches. Taste the beans and if they are almost tender, add 1 tablespoon salt; if they are not, do not add the salt yet. Return to high heat, cover, and bring to a boil. Reduce the heat to low, cover partially, and simmer until the beans are completely tender but not mushy, about 30 minutes; if you did not add the salt, check the beans for tenderness every 10–15 minutes and add 1 tablespoon salt when they are almost tender. Drain well.

## chopping or dicing onions

*1 Halve and peel the onion* Using a sharp chef's knife, cut the sprout end off of the onion. Set the onion on the cut side, and then halve it lengthwise from the root end to the sprout end. Peel away and discard the papery outer skin from each half.

*2 Make a series of lengthwise cuts* Set one onion half flat side down on a cutting board. Make a series of lengthwise cuts from the sprout end to the root end, but do not cut all the way through the root end.

*3 Make a series of horizontal cuts* Next, position the root end of the onion half to the left if you are right-handed or to the right if you are left-handed. With the knife blade held parallel with the board, make a series of parallel vertical cuts from the sprout end, stopping short of the root end.

*4 Chop or dice the onion* Finally, make a series of cuts perpendicular to the first two sets of cuts, working from the sprout end to the root end. Repeat steps 2 through 4 with the remaining onion half.

## working with fresh herbs

**cilantro, dill, mint, parsley, tarragon, sage** Pluck the leaves from the stems. Gather the leaves into a pile on a cutting board and then rock a chef's knife back and forth over them until they are of the desired fineness.

**thyme and rosemary** To remove the leaves, gently run your thumb and index finger down the stems, against the direction of the leaves' growth. Leaves that are firmly attached to the stem will require plucking. Gather the leaves into a pile on a cutting board and then rock a chef's knife back and forth over them until they are of the desired fineness.

**chives** Gather the chives into a small bundle on a cutting board. Using a sharp chef's knife, cut the chives crosswise into small pieces. Alternatively, chives can be snipped with kitchen scissors.

## working with citrus

**zesting** If a recipe calls for both citrus zest and juice, zest the fruit before juicing because it is easier to zest when it is whole. To grate citrus zest, use a fine-toothed rasp-style grater. Using light pressure, move the citrus back and forth against the grater's teeth, removing only the colored rind and leaving behind the white pith, which is bitter tasting. For large strips, use a sharp vegetable peeler to remove the zest in long, wide pieces, working from pole to pole.

**juicing** To get the most juice from a citrus fruit, it helps if the fruit is at room temperature. Just before juicing, roll it back and forth along the work surface under the palm of your hand, applying firm pressure, so that the fruit softens slightly. Cut the fruit in half and use a citrus press or reamer to squeeze the juice from each half. Strain the juice to remove seeds and bits of pulp.

## seeding cucumbers

*1 Halve the cucumber* Peel the cucumber, if the recipe directs. Using a chef's knife, cut the cucumber in half lengthwise.

*2 Scoop out the seeds* Using the rounded tip of a soup spoon, scrape out the seeds from each cucumber half.

## cutting corn off the cob

*1 Remove the husks* Pull off and discard the husks and silks from each ear of corn.

*2 Cut each cob in half* Using a chef's knife, cut each cob in half crosswise.

*3 Cut the kernels off the cob* Stand one half of the cob on a cut side on the cutting board. With the knife blade held close against the cob, slice the kernels off the cob. Rotate the the cob, as needed, until all the kernels have been cut away.

## cleaning fresh mushrooms

*1 Brush or wipe away the dirt* Using a mushroom brush or damp cloth, gently brush or wipe away any dirt from the mushrooms.

*2 Trim the stems* Using a paring knife, trim a thin slice from the base of the stem of each mushroom. Or, if only the mushroom caps are needed, cut or break off the entire stem.

## working with shrimp

*1 Peel the shrimp* Pull off the legs from the underside of each shrimp. Starting from the head end, peel away the shell. If desired, leave the tail and the shell segment closest to it attached.

*2 Remove the veins* Using a sharp paring knife, make a shallow cut along the outer curve of each shrimp. If there is a dark vein running along the length of the shrimp, lift it out with the tip of the knife.

## pitting olives

*1 Crush the olives* Place the olives in a zipper-lock plastic bag, force out the air, and seal closed. Using a meat pounder or rolling pin, gently crush the olives until the flesh splits open. Alternatively, press on the olives with the flat side of a chef's knife.

*2 Remove the pits* Remove the crushed olives from the bag and separate the pits from the olive flesh with your fingers. Use a paring knife to cut the flesh from the pits of any stubborn olives.

## puréeing soups

**using an immersion blender** An immersion, or stick, blender is an easy way to purée soups because it can be used directly in the pot that the mixture was cooked in, eliminating the need to dirty additional bowls or equipment. The drawback, however, is that an immersion blender, at best, creates a purée with a coarse, slightly pulpy texture.

**using a standing blender** A standing blender yields a fine purée, but puréeing hot liquids in one requires caution: The pressure created by steam can cause the lid to pop off when the blender is turned on. Before puréeing hot liquids, allow the mixture to cool for a few minutes. Purée in batches, leaving at least 2 inches of room at the top of the blender jar each time you fill it. If the lid has a removable handle or knob, take out that piece, cover the jar with the lid, and then hold it in place with a kitchen towel before turning on the motor. Start the blender on low and gradually increase the speed.

## seasoning soups

Homemade stock or broth is always the best-tasting choice for soup if you have the time to make it. Purchased broth is an alternative to homemade in many of the recipes in this book, but be sure to use low-sodium broth; this allows you to have better control over the amount of salt that goes into the dish. Before serving soup, remember to taste it and, if needed, adjust the seasonings with salt, pepper, and, in some cases, with vinegar, lemon juice, soy sauce, or other salty or acidic ingredients. This step is especially important with a chilled soup because once cold, it tastes much less seasoned than it did when it was warm or at room temperature.

## keeping soups hot or cold for serving

**hot soups** To keep a hot soup hot, even after it's been brought to the table, it's a good idea to warm the serving bowls. One way to do this is to put the bowls in a 200°F oven (make sure that the bowls are heatproof) for a few minutes. Another way is to pour scalding water into them. Let them stand for about 5 minutes, then pour out the water and wipe the bowls before ladling in the hot soup.

**cold soups** To keep a cold soup cold once it's served, chill the bowls ahead of time by placing them in the freezer or refrigerator. If freezer or refrigerator space is at a premium, pour ice water into the bowls and let them stand on the countertop for 5–10 minutes. Before ladling in the soup, pour out the ice water and wipe out the bowls.

## storing soups

Most soups keep well. The exceptions are soups made with uncooked ingredients, such as gazpacho, and soups with very starchy components, such as tomato and bread soup. To store soup, transfer it to an airtight container and let it cool completely, uncovered, then cover it tightly and refrigerate. To reheat soup, tranfer it to a saucepan and heat it gently over medium heat. If the soup has thickened upon standing (soups with starchy ingredients are particularly susceptible), stir in addtional broth until it reaches the desired consistency. Be sure to taste the soup and adjust the seasonings, if needed.

# seasonal ingredients

All produce has a peak season when the taste is as good as it gets. The chart at right indicates the seasonality of most of the types of produce used in this book. Note that though some fruits and vegetables, such as apples and eggplants, are available thoughout the year, they do have seasons when they are at their peak. Solid dots indicate peak seasons; open dots indicate transitional seasons.

| INGREDIENTS | SPRING | SUMMER | FALL | WINTER |
|---|:---:|:---:|:---:|:---:|
| apples, granny smith | | | ● | ○ |
| artichokes | ● | | ● | |
| arugula | ● | ● | ● | |
| asparagus | ● | | | |
| avocados | ● | ● | ● | ● |
| beans, fava | ● | | | |
| beans, green | | ● | | |
| beets | | ● | ● | ○ |
| bok choy, baby | ● | | ● | ● |
| butternut squash | | | ● | ● |
| cabbage, napa | ● | ● | ● | ● |
| carrots | ● | ○ | ● | ● |
| cauliflower | | ● | ● | ○ |
| celery root | | | ● | ● |
| cherries, sour | ● | | | |
| cherries, sweet | ○ | ● | | |
| chestnuts | | | ● | ● |
| chiles, fresh | | ● | ● | |
| cucumbers | | ● | | |
| eggplant | | ● | ○ | |
| fennel | ● | ● | ● | ● |

| INGREDIENTS | SPRING | SUMMER | FALL | WINTER |
|---|---|---|---|---|
| garlic | | ● | ○ | |
| green garlic | ● | | | |
| kale | ○ | ○ | ● | ● |
| leeks | ● | ● | ● | ● |
| lemons | ○ | | | ● |
| limes | ○ | | | ● |
| mushrooms, cremini | ● | ● | ● | ● |
| onions, sweet | ● | | | |
| oranges | ○ | | | ● |
| pears | | | ● | ● |
| peppers, bell | | ● | ● | |
| potatoes | ○ | | ● | ● |
| shallots | | ● | ● | ○ |
| spinach, baby | ● | ● | ● | ● |
| squash, summer | | ● | ○ | |
| sweet potatoes | | | ● | ● |
| swiss chard | ● | ● | ● | ● |
| tomatillos | | ● | ● | |
| tomatoes | | ● | ○ | |
| watercress | ● | | ● | ● |
| zucchini | | ● | ○ | |

# glossary

**aioli** A pungent garlic-flavored mayonnaise, aioli is a classic sauce and condiment popular in the south of France.

**apple cider, hard** This bubbly beverage is apple juice or cider that has been allowed to ferment and develop alcohol.

**applejack** This brandy made from apples has a deep amber color. Its flavor is slightly sweet, with the distinct flavor of apples.

**arugula** The leaves of this dark green plant, also called rocket, resemble deeply notched, elongated oak leaves. They have a nutty, tangy, and slightly peppery flavor. Mature arugula is often more pungent than mild, tender baby arugula.

**bamboo shoots** Used frequently in Asian cooking, bamboo shoots have a crunchy texture and a pleasant, mildly sweet flavor. They are commonly sold in cans or jars.

**beans, dried** There is a wide variety of dried beans in markets today. The two types used in this book are discussed below.

*black* Black beans are small in size. They are sometimes called turtle beans and have a firm, dense texture and a mild, slightly sweet flavor when cooked.

*pinto* These pale brown beans sometimes have spots or streaks of color that disappear with cooking. They have a full, earthy flavor and creamy texture.

**beans, fava** Also called broad beans, this springtime bean has an earthy, slightly bitter flavor. The edible portion must be removed from the large outer pod, and then each bean must be slipped out of its tough skin.

**bisque** A rich soup with a thick, smooth texture, bisque is often made with shellfish as the primary ingredient. The thickener in a classic bisque is rice that is cooked into the base and puréed with the other ingredients.

**blade steak, beef** A cut from the chuck, or shoulder, of the cow, blade steak is sometimes labeled "flat iron steak." It has a thick line of gristle running along its length that should be trimmed away before cooking.

**bonito flakes** These delicate, buff-colored, almost translucent flakes are shaved from a bonito fish that has been dried and smoked. The shavings have a subtle smoky fish taste and aroma, and are one of the principal ingredients in Japanese dipping sauces and *dashi*, a traditional fish stock.

**broth** A liquid that is made by cooking vegetables, poultry, meat, or seafood in water is called a broth. No matter the primary flavoring, broth is seasoned with salt, whereas stock is not. If using store-bought broth, seek out low-sodium versions.

**Calvados** This oak-aged apple brandy comes from Normandy, France, where it is sipped as a digestif as well as used in both sweet and savory dishes.

**celery root** Also known as celeriac, celery root is a round, knobby fall and winter vegetable that contributes a subtle celery flavor when cooked and a crisp crunch to salads when used raw.

**celery seed** This tiny dried seed of the wild celery plant has a strong celery flavor and is often used in potato salad, coleslaw, and pickling mixtures.

**cheese** Cheese adds unique flavor and texture to many dishes, including soups. To ensure freshness, purchase cheese from a specialty cheese shop.

*Asiago* This cow's-milk cheese from northern Italy is an excellent melting cheese. Young Asiago, sometimes called fresh Asiago, has a semifirm texture and a mildly, slightly nutty flavor. Aged Asiago has a pleasantly sharp flavor and dry texture that makes it suitable for grating.

*blue* Blue cheeses have been treated with mold and have formed bluish veins or pockets of mold that give the cheese its strong, piquant flavor. They range in texture from dry and crumbly to soft and creamy.

*Cheddar, English* First made in the village of Cheddar, England, this cow's-milk cheese is appreciated for its rich, salty flavor, which ranges from mild to sharp, depending on age. For soup, look for a true English Cheddar with a bold, sharp taste.

*cotija* This dry, crumbly Mexican cow's-milk cheese has an assertive saltiness but otherwise a very mild flavor. It is not typically served as table cheese; most often, it is crumbled over soups, tacos, beans, and vegetables as a lightly piquant flavor accent. Cotija is sometimes sold as *queso añejo* or *queso seco*.

*goat, fresh* Also called *chèvre*, this pure white cheese is made from goat's milk and has a soft texture and a pleasantly tangy, slightly salty flavor. Do not use aged goat cheese in a recipe calling for fresh.

*feta* A white, crumbly sheep's or cow's milk cheese that is cured in brine, feta is a traditional Greek cheese, though it is now made in many countries, including the United States and France. It has a salty, tangy flavor.

*Parmigiano-Reggiano* This true Parmesan cheese is made from cow's milk in northern Italy according to strict standards. Versions made in other countries are also available, but none can match the rich, nutty, and complex flavor of Parmigiano-Reggiano.

**chestnuts, steamed peeled** Fresh chestnuts are sold in their smooth, mahogany-colored shells. They are very labor-intensive to cook and peel for use as an ingredient in a dish. Fortunately, steamed and peeled chestnuts are sold in jars in some grocery stores and specialty food stores, especially in the fall and winter. Chestnuts have a mild sweetness and meaty, starchy texture.

**chickpeas** Also known as garbanzo beans or *ceci* beans, these rich, nutty-flavored beans are beige in color, round in shape, and have a firm texture.

**chile garlic paste, Asian** This bright red-orange condiment is made from ground fresh chiles and is seasoned with garlic. It is sold in jars in well-stocked supermarkets and Asian grocery stores.

**chiles** When buying fresh chiles, seek out plump, firm, unblemished specimens. When shopping for dried chiles, look for ones that are soft and pliant, not hard and brittle.

*ancho* Ancho chiles are the dried form of fresh poblano chiles. They are broad at the shoulders and taper to a point. Burgundy-black in color, anchos taste of dried fruits and chocolate, and have little to no heat.

*chipotle chiles in adobo sauce* Chipotle chiles are ripe red jalapeños that have been smoked. To make chipotle chiles in adobo, they are packed in a vinegary seasoned tomato sauce. Chipotle chiles in adobo are sold canned in most supermarkets.

*jalapeño* This bright green chile, averaging about 2 inches in length, ranges from hot to very hot and is one of the the most widely used chiles in the United States.

*poblano* Deep green with broad shoulders and a tapered body, a poblano chile is about 5 inches long. It is only mildly hot and has a green, earthy flavor. Poblano chiles that are dried are known as ancho chiles.

*serrano* Serrano chiles are slightly smaller in size than jalapeños, but typically have a little more heat. They are often sold in their green state, although red serrano chiles are sometimes available.

**chili powder** This spice blend combines dried chiles, cumin, oregano, garlic, with other spices. It is often used in the cooking of the American Southwest, but is never used in authentic Mexican cooking. Do not mistake chili powder with pure ground chile powder, which is simply dried chile pods ground into a fine powder.

**chorizo, Spanish** A coarse pork sausage seasoned with garlic and paprika, Spanish chorizo is often cured, dried, or smoked, and has a tangy flavor. Before use, its casing must be removed. Do not substitute Mexican chorizo, a fresh sausage, for Spanish chorizo.

**coconut** The fruit of a tropical palm, coconuts have many culinary uses. Three types of coconut products are used in this book.

*unsweetened shredded coconut* These fine dried shreds come from the white inner meat of the coconut. Look for them in natural-foods stores or Asian markets.

*light unsweetened coconut milk* This lower-fat version of coconut milk has a slightly thinner texture and a leaner flavor than regular coconut milk, but is suitable for many recipes calling for coconut milk.

*unsweetened coconut milk* Sold in cans, coconut milk is made by processing grated coconut meat and water. Upon standing, the coconut fat rises to the surface of the milk, so, before use, shake the can or stir the contents well.

**crab, King** This large species of crab is harvested in the cold waters off of Alaska. The legs are the meatiest part of this crab; they are sold cooked and frozen in many grocery stores.

**cucumber, English** Slender, dark green English cucumbers, also called hothouse or hydroponic cucumbers, have thinner skins and fewer seeds than regular cucumbers. They are often sold shrink-wrapped in plastic alongside regular cucumbers.

**curry paste, Thai** Curry pastes are complex blends of chiles, shallots, garlic, herbs, and spices that are flavor bases for Thai curries. Look for them in small jars or cans in well-stocked grocery stores and Asian markets.

*red* Spicy Thai red curry paste is made from a mixture of dried red chiles, garlic, cilantro, lemongrass, shallots, shrimp paste, and other seasonings and spices.

*yellow* Thai yellow curry paste gets it yellowish color and earthy flavor from an abundance of turmeric. It is only mildly spicy.

**curry powder** Curry powder is a convenience product meant to simplify the daily chore of blending spices for Indian cooks. It is a complex mixture of numerous ground chiles, spices, seeds, and herbs.

**dashi** This basic broth is one of the building blocks of Japanese cuisine. It is made with bonito flakes, *kombu*, and water. *Dashi* should be clear and have a subtle, slightly smoky, lightly fishy flavor.

**edamame** Green soybeans often go by their Japanese name, edamame. They are sold frozen, both in their pods and shelled.

**farro** This variety of wheat is also sometimes known as emmer. It is considered to have ancient origins and was, at one time, popular in Mediterranean and Middle Eastern cuisines. Today, it is used most notably in Italian cooking. The grain's cooked texture is quite chewy and and its flavor is nutty and wholesome.

**fish sauce, Asian** Made from salted and fermented fish, fish sauce is a thin, clear liquid that ranges in color from amber to dark brown. Southeast Asians use it in the same way Westerners use salt, both as a cooking ingredient and as a seasoning at the table.

**gazpacho** This classic chilled soup hails from Andalusia in southern Spain. Typically, it is a puréed soup with a tomato base that incorporates many summer vegetables as well as olive oil and bread crumbs.

**green garlic** Immature garlic shoots, stalks of green garlic resemble green onions. They taste of mature garlic, but without its pungency or harshness. They are available only in the spring.

**gremolata** This Italian herb condiment is a simple mixture of minced parsley, lemon zest, and garlic. A traditional garnish for osso buco, gremolata adds bright, fresh flavor to any dish to which it is added.

**hominy** These are dried corn kernels have been soaked in alkali such as slaked lime or lye, washed to remove the outer skin, and then cooked. They resemble soft, white, rather puffed-up kernels of corn. Hominy is sold dried or ready-to-eat in cans.

**kombu** This type of dried sea kelp is fundamental to Japanese cuisine. It is usually sold in thin, dark-green sheets that are covered with a white salt residue and have a strong sea-like aroma. Its most common use is as a flavoring for *dashi*, the broth used to make miso soup.

**lemongrass** This herb with a fresh lemon flavor, but with none of lemon's brassiness, resembles a green onion with pale green leaves. The tender inner core contains the most flavor.

**lentils, French green** Also called Puy lentils, these tiny green-gray lentils have a mottled appearance. Their flavor is mild and earthy, and they tend to retain their shape with cooking more so than other lentil varieties.

**maple syrup, grade b pure** Maple syrup is made by boiling down the sap of the sugar maple tree to an amber-colored syrup. The syrup is graded according to color. Cooking maple and grade B are the darkest in color and have robust flavor; grade A syrup has a lighter color and flavor.

**matzoh meal** Matzoh meal is ground from unleavened matzoh bread that is traditionally eaten at Passover. Like bread crumbs, matzoh meal is used to bind, thicken, and coat other foods, as well as for making matzoh balls.

**merguez sausage** Made from lamb, merguez is a spicy fresh sausage originally from North Africa. Its red color comes from the spices and chiles that flavor it.

**minestra** The Italian word for "soup," minestra has come to be known as a soup of moderate heartiness, often featuring vegetables.

**mirin** An important ingredient in Japanese cooking, mirin is a sweet cooking wine made by fermenting glutinous rice and sugar. The pale gold and syrupy wine adds a rich flavor and translucent sheen to sauces, dressings, and simmered dishes.

**miso, white** A staple of the Japanese kitchen, miso is a fermented paste of soybeans and grain. Relatively mild-tasting white miso, or *shiro* miso, is one of the more common varieties. Look for miso in the refrigerator case of well-stocked grocery or natural foods stores, or in Japanese markets.

**mushrooms** A wide array of mushroom varieties is available to cooks these days. Each type has a unique flavor and texture.

*cremini* Resembling white button mushrooms in shape and size, cremini are mottled brown in color. They have a firmer texture and fuller flavor than white mushrooms.

*porcini, dried* Dried porcini mushrooms are sold in well-stocked grocery stores and specialty markets. They have an intensely savory aroma and flavor. When cooking with them, just a small amount adds a full, woodsy flavor. When buying, look for packages with large pieces and very few small, crumbly bits.

*shiitake, dried* Originally from Japan, shiitake mushrooms are now widely available in the U.S. Dried shiitakes have a very earthy, meaty aroma and flavor. Look for those with pale cracks in the caps' surfaces.

**nonreactive** Untreated aluminum or cast iron pans can react with acidic ingredients such as citrus juice, vinegar, or wine, giving them a metallic flavor and an off color. When in doubt, choose stainless steel, anodized aluminum, or enameled cast iron for pans cooking or stainless steel, glass, or ceramic bowls for mixing acidic mixtures.

**oils** Some oils are best used for high-heat cooking, some for drizzling over a finished dish as a flavor accent.

*canola* This neutral-tasting oil is pressed from rapeseed, a relative of the mustard plant. High in monounsaturated fat, it is good for general cooking. It also has a high smoking point and can be used for frying.

*chili oil, Asian* This oil, available in Asian markets and many supermarkets, is made by steeping hot chiles in neutral-tasting vegetable oil. The chiles infuse the oil with a vibrant red color and a searing spiciness.

*olive* The first cold pressing of olives yields extra-virgin olive oil, the variety that is the lowest in acid and the purest, with a flavor that reflects where the olives were grown. Extra-virgin olive oil is best used in preparations in which it is not subjected to high heat, which destroys its flavor. Subsequent pressing yields plain "olive oil" that is suitable for general cooking.

*sesame, Asian* This dark-colored oil is pressed from toasted sesame seeds. It has a strong flavor and should be used sparingly as a seasoning in Asian-inspired dishes.

**olives, Kalamata** Salty, brine-cured Kalamata olives are named after the city of Kalamata in southern Greece. These black olives have a dark purple hue; they are large in size with a strong, pungent flavor and a slight fruitiness.

**orzo** The Italian word for "barley," this pasta shape resembles large, flat grains of rice. It is particulary well-suited for use in soups.

**Pernod** This brightly colored yellowish-green anise-flavored liqueur is popular in France, where it is made. It is often sipped mixed with water as an aperitif.

**pumpkin purée** This thick, unflavored purée of cooked pumpkin, sometimes simply labeled as pumpkin, is sold in cans. When buying, take care not to mistake pumpkin pie filling, which is seasoned with spices, for pumpkin purée.

**pumpkin seeds, shelled** Also called *pepitas*, shelled pumpkin seeds are green in color and have a slightly vegetal and nutty flavor.

**quinoa** An staple of the ancient Incas of Peru, this highly nutritious grain looks like spherical sesame seeds. When cooked, quinoa has a mild taste and light, fluffy texture. It must be rinsed well before cooking because the grain has a natural residue that is very bitter tasting.

**rice** The most widely eaten of all grains, different varieties of rice have unique characteristics. The two types used in this book as discussed below.

*basmati* Basmati rice is an aromatic long-grain rice with a very nutty flavor and fragrance. It is the favored rice of India and parts of the Middle East.

*jasmine* Similar to basmati, jasmine rice is an aromatic long-grain variety with a nutty, faintly floral flavor. It is Thai in origin.

**rice wine, Chinese** Also known as Shaoxing wine, Chinese rice wine is made from glutinous rice and is used for both cooking and sipping. Look for it in Asian grocery stores.

**roux** A mixture of flour and fat (often butter or oil), roux is used as a thickener for sauces, soups and stews. How long the roux is cooked determines its color. Lightly cooked white or blond roux has little flavor and the most thickening power. Brown roux results from long cooking; it has a deep, toasty flavor, but has less thickening power.

**saffron** Saffron is the stigma of a small crocus that is hand-picked and then dried. It takes several thousand flowers to yield just 1 ounce of dried saffron threads, explaining saffron's status as the most expensive spice. Luckily, a little goes a long way; just a pinch is all that is needed to season foods and lend a saffron's characteristic golden yellow hue.

**serrano ham** A dry-cured ham made in mountainous areas of Spain. Although similar to Italian prosciutto, a side-by-side tasting would show subtle but distinct differences in flavor and texture.

**sherry, dry** A fortified wine originating in southern Spain, sherry is made from the Palomino Fino grape. Dry sherry is mild in sweetness and is often used in cooking.

**soba noodles, buckwheat** These grayish beige Japanese noodles have square-cut edges and a nutty, earthy flavor that comes from the buckwheat flour that is used to make them. They can be served in hot or cold preparations. Most often, soba is sold dried in packages containing small bundles.

**smoked paprika** A Spanish specialty, smoked paprika is made from red chiles that have been smoked and then ground. It has a very earthy, smoky, and almost meaty flavor and a deep red color. Smoked paprika is available in sweet or mild (*dulce*), bittersweet (*agridulce*), and hot (*picante*) varieties.

**star anise** These deep-brown star-shaped pods have a flavor much like that of their namesake, anise seed, but with a more savory and assertive quality. They are native to China and, ground into powder, are a component in Chinese five-spice powder.

**stock** Like broth, stock is made by simmering vegetables, poultry, meat, or seafood in water. But, unlike broth, stock is not seasoned with salt because it is often the foundation for sauces that are made by reduction, which concentrates the flavorings.

**tofu, extra-firm** High in protein and very mild in flavor, tofu is simply soybean curd. Extra-firm tofu has the densest texture of all the varieties. Tofu is most commonly sold packed in water and should be drained and rinsed before use.

**tomatillos** Tomatillos resemble small, firm green tomatoes enclosed in a papery husk. Their flavor is faintly fruity and tart, with a slight vegetal quality. Before use, peel off and discard the husks and rinse the tomatillos to wash away the sticky residue on the skins.

**vinegars** Each type of vinegar has a unique flavor profile and acidity that makes it particularly suited to certain preparations.

*balsamic* A specialty of the Italian region of Emilia-Romagna, balsamic vinegar is an aged vinegar made from the unfermented grape juice, or must, of Trebbiano grapes. Aged in a series of wooden casks of decreasing sizes, each of a different wood, balsamic grows sweeter and more mellow with time.

*Chinese black* This dark vinegar is made by fermenting grain, often glutinous rice, millet, barley, wheat, sorghum, or some combination thereof. Its flavor is malty, slightly smoky, and has a touch of sweetness.

*raspberry* Flowery and sweet, this vinegar is made from white wine vinegar flavored and colored by the addition of raspberries.

*red wine* Sharply acidic, red wine vinegar is produced when red wine is fermented for a second time.

*rice* Popular in Asian cooking, rice vinegar is a clear, mild, and slightly sweet vinegar produced from fermented glutinous rice. It is available

plain or sweetened; the latter is marketed as seasoned rice vinegar.

*sherry* True sherry vinegar from Spain, labeled "vinagre de Jerez," has a slightly sweet, nutty taste, a result of aging in oak.

*white wine* Light in flavor and pale in color, this vinegar can be produced from a variety of white wines, such as Chardonnay or Sauvignon Blanc.

**vermouth, dry** This fortified wine is infused with herbs and spices. It is available in sweet (red) and dry (white) varieties. Dry white vermouth is an ingredient in a classic martini and is often used in cooking.

**watercress** This member of the mustard family has round, deep-green leaves on delicate stems. Watercress has a refreshing, peppery flavor that turns bitter with age.

**yogurt, Greek-style** This style of yogurt has a thick, creamy texture and a rich, tangy flavor. If it is not available, a reasonable substitute can be made by placing plain whole-milk yogurt in a cheesecloth-lined fine-mesh sieve and allowing it to drain for a few hours.

# index

**OXMOOR HOUSE**

Oxmoor House books are distributed by Sunset Books
80 Willow Road, Menlo Park, CA 94025
Telephone: 650 324 1532
VP and Associate Publisher  Jim Childs
Director of Marketing  Sydney Webber
Oxmoor House and Sunset Books are divisions
of Southern Progress Corporation

**WILLIAMS-SONOMA, INC.**

Founder & Vice-Chairman  Chuck Williams

**WILLIAMS-SONOMA NEW FLAVORS SERIES**

Conceived and produced by Weldon Owen Inc.
415 Jackson Street, Suite 200, San Francisco, CA 94111
Telephone: 415 291 0100 Fax: 415 291 8841
www.weldonowen.com

In Collaboration with Williams-Sonoma, Inc.
3250 Van Ness Avenue, San Francisco, CA 94109

A WELDON OWEN PRODUCTION

First printed in 2009
Printed in Singapore

Printed by Tien Wah Press
10 9 8 7 6 5 4 3 2 1
Library of Congress Cataloging-in-Publication Data is available.

ISBN-13: 978-0-8487-3271-4
ISBN-10: 0-8487-3271-5

**WELDON OWEN INC.**

Executive Chairman, Weldon Owen Group  John Owen
CEO and President, Weldon Owen Inc.  Terry Newell
Senior VP, International Sales  Stuart Laurence
VP, Sales and New Business Development  Amy Kaneko
Director of Finance  Mark Perrigo

VP and Publisher  Hannah Rahill
Executive Editor  Jennifer Newens
Senior Editor  Dawn Yanagihara

VP and Creative Director  Gaye Allen
Art Director  Kara Church
Senior Designer  Ashley Martinez
Designer  Stephanie Tang
Photo Manager  Meghan Hildebrand

Production Director  Chris Hemesath
Production Manager  Michelle Duggan
Color Manager  Teri Bell

Photographer  Kate Sears
Food Stylist  Shelly Kaldunski
Prop Stylist  Danielle Fisher

Additional Photography Tucker + Hossler: pages 24, 33, 45, 55, 60, 69, 73, 81, 86, 89, 94, 101, 102, 113, 118, 126, 129, 141; Getty Images: Tom Hopkins pages 14–15; Louis-Laurent Grandadam pages 46–47; Justin Lightley page 116; Corbis: Ed Young page 53; Veer: Somos Photography page 59; Westend61 Photography pages 78–79; Fotosearch: Photographers Choice page 75; Creatas Photos page 107; Westend61 Photography pages 110–111

ACKNOWLEDGMENTS

Weldon Owen wishes to thank the following individuals for their kind assistance: Photo Assistants Victoria Wall and Tony George; Food Stylist Assistants Lillian Kang and Ara Armstrong; Copy editor Carrie Bradley; Proofreader Lesli Neilson; Indexer Ken DellaPenta.